Letters

of
Unconditional Love

Inspired by six years of weekly
Letters from Kenneth Wapnick, Ph.D.

Bunny Moazed MS

BALBOA
PRESS
A DIVISION OF HAY HOUSE

Balboa Press books may be ordered through booksellers or by contacting:

Balboa Press
A Division of Hay House
1663 Liberty Drive
Bloomington, IN 47403
www.balboapress.com
1 (877) 407-4847

Print information available on the last page.

ISBN: 978-1-5043-5470-7 (sc)
ISBN: 978-1-5043-5471-4 (e)

Library of Congress Control Number: 2016937785

Balboa Press rev. date: 09/15/2016

Dedication

*L*etters of Unconditional Love: Based on the book, *A Course in Miracles,* is dedicated to Tamara Morgan, *The Foundation for Inner Peace.* Tamara had the vision to recognize the value of telling our story and encouraged me, in a loving way, to do so. How I learned to accept the concept of Unconditional Love through six years of weekly letters from Kenneth Wapnick Ph.D. Letters of Unconditional Love ~ is intended to be an inspiration to current and future students of *A Course in Miracles.* Most of all they represent an *Attitude of Gratitude* to Kenneth Wapnick Ph.D. who never, ever, gave up on me!

Epigraph

*R*evelation unites you directly with God. Miracles unite you directly with your brother. Neither emanates from Consciousness, but both are experienced there. Revelation is intensely personal and cannot be meaningfully translated. Revelation is literally unspeakable because it is an experience of unspeakable love. Miracles, however are genuinely interpersonal and result in true closeness to others. *A Course in Miracles,* (T-1, II: 1-2).

Preface

*I*n 2003, I joined a study group on *A Course in Miracles* (ACIM) at the Unity Church in Burbank, CA. This came about after investigating several other philosophies and deciding ACIM was the one. Shortly after, the facilitator transferred out of state leaving me in charge of the class.

It was terrifying to be in charge and still not understanding the Course that well, however I rationalized all I really had to do was show up on time, open the church, turn on the lights, bring water, and then we read. As it turned out, that was just the beginning!

I loved the Course' sophisticated writing style and even if I did not understand every word, there was something about it that kept me engaged. I wanted to understand it! This became my Thursday evening social group and I looked forward to each class.

One evening a student questioned the concept, "when we slip into the ego we perpetuate the illusion." It sounded hopeless, and I did not have an answer. For some reason, I decided to write Kenneth Wapnick Ph.D. and President of the Foundation for *A Course in Miracles* and ask for clarification. I did so without any anticipation of the results. If he responded, we had the answer – If he did not respond - the students were not aware I had written to Dr. Wapnick, anyway.

Never in my wildest dreams could I have imagined how that one 'goofy letter' would initiate weekly letters from Dr. Wapnick for the next six years: and change my life forever! Tamara encouraged me to write a book because the letters highlighted Dr. Wapnick's playful persona not usually demonstrated during his serious Course Lectures… In the process, a whole new and fabulous concept has emerged!

Introduction

Shortly before my first letter to Dr. Wapnick I was in a horrendous accident and broke my neck. I had to sleep propped up and sometimes this meant downstairs on my ottoman. One night I was awaken by the most beautiful dream – it was as if an angel was talking to me without saying any words, yet I understood everything he said. When the Entity faded out my first reaction was, "Holy-Moly what was that?"

In my next letter I related my recent dream while asleep on the 'holy-moly' and was surprised to learn Ken already knew of it. I had to read his confirmation of this visit several times before the impact of his confession sunk-in. This changed everything I had ever thought about the Course, and every thought I would be thinking in the future!

Ken's revelation opened a whole new dimension and not just to the Course. The impact on my life, my understanding of the Course, and my friendship with Ken were about to change, forever. I was excited about having his visit confirmed, yet speechless and confused over how to process this information. I seemed to be suspended temporarily from reality and held within a series of beautiful thoughts.

Originally, Tamara convinced me to tell our story to demonstrate Ken's personable side, whereas the real story is far beyond what is known about Ken. When Ken wrote 'I was the only one who ever met with him on the Holy-Moly' it can only mean one thing – Ken traveled outside the body – and confirms this in his letters!

We continued to meet frequently - as one-in-spirit - where Ken transferred his unconditional love into my lack-of-love until I recognized unconditional love belonged to me, also. "When spirits original state of direct communication is reached, neither the body, nor the miracle serves any purpose," (T-1, V-2).

Ken taught the meaning of unconditional love by living it. I am overwhelmed with gratitude that Ken saw something in me making me worthy of sharing his ability to enjoy the very concepts he taught through his lectures.

The following is our Story ~

Contents

Dedication v

Epigraph vii

Preface ix

Introduction xi

The Ultimate Gift 1

My Big-Bang! 20

Chalk & Cheese 27

ACIM ~ Baggins & Fogg Books 41

A Course in Miracles - OBE & NDE 46

ACIM & Einstein's E = MC ^{2} 51

Kenneth Wapnick Ph.D. & Freud 60

Chunky Monkey 74

A Tribute to Ken 77

Literary Hug for My Cherished Friend 84

The Little Garden 86

References 97

Epilogue 99

Reader's Guide 101

About the Author 105

1

The Ultimate Gift

Teach only love for that is what you are.
(T-6, I-13:2).

*T*his is not a story about *me* and *my* letters from Kenneth Wapnick, Ph.D. This is my story about how Dr. Wapnick's letters taught me the true meaning of Unconditional Love, a concept from the book, *A Course in Miracles* (ACIM). How I chattered away with what I called 'goofy-letters' to this gifted and erudite professional, and why he bothered to respond is what I call a miracle! Did I understand what Ken was doing – of course not! Nor did I understand why Ken continued to respond to my goofy-letters!

The uniqueness of our letters is not just that Ken responded because Ken took the time to respond to everyone who wrote to him: it probably was not in the volume of letters because Ken had been around nearly 30 years before we began corresponding: It was certainly not in his way of expressing love because he was total love for everyone with whom he came into contact: It had to do with Ken recognizing in me what I could not see in myself and staying with me until I got-it! I call this: *The Ultimate Gift!*

"While you believe you are in a body you can choose between loveless and miraculous channels of expression. You can make an empty shell, but you cannot express nothing at all. You can wait, delay, paralyze yourself, or reduce your creativity almost to nothing. But, you cannot abolish it. You can destroy your medium of communication, but not your potential. You did not create yourself." (T-1, V-1: 3-8).

Writing a letter to Kenneth Wapnick Ph.D. seemed perfectly logical, at the time. As facilitator for *A Course in Miracles* my study group had a question and I needed the answer, so I wrote to Dr. Wapnick. It is not likely I would have written if not for the fact as facilitator I was supposed to know this stuff. Besides, I learned long ago: if you have a question – where do you go? To the Source of Course!

In the event Dr. Wapnick responded we would have the answer to our question. In the meantime, we were not waiting for a reply, in fact, I had not told the class I had written to the President of the Foundation for *A Course in Miracles*!

Why Dr. Wapnick continued to write - came to mind on many occasions. It was not like I had been a long-time Course student and thus ready for some sort of transition. I was raised on fire and brimstone: did not go to church for 30 years after my only son was killed in a hit-and-run: kicked out of a Black church after more than two-years: and fired from my job when I was 66 for taking a screenplay to a studio on my day off! As corny as this last event sounds it gave me time to explore a variety of philosophies before settling on ACIM in 2003.

In the Autumn of 2003 I became facilitator for *A Course in Miracles,* (ACIM) and did not understand most of it. Yet, I knew I wanted to understand it before I either accepted or rejected the

Course concepts! A few of us from our study group decided to visit Dr. Wapnick at the ACIM Foundation in Temecula, and take in his lecture for a little clarification. During a break I met Dr. Wapnick in passing and told him I loved the Blue book. He took my face in both hands, kissed my cheek, told me to read it again, and disappeared into the crowd.

This very brief encounter was to be the first and only time we met in person. We never spoke again after our brief conversation during the break, nor did we exchange names and numbers, or ever speak on the phone, analog or otherwise. To think Ken would remember me four years later when I wrote the first letter is a giant stretch, even for someone as gifted as Ken.

On May 19, 2007 my vehicle was struck by a City bus running a red light, spun around and struck again throwing my vehicle 33 feet into a stone building breaking my neck. This event changed everything - except my weekly meetings as a facilitator for ACIM. Three months later I wrote to Dr. Wapnick with my question generating weekly letters from Ken until he passed in 2013.

During the six years of weekly letters I never mentioned to anyone we were corresponding, nor hinted to other Course students about letters from Ken. It seemed almost impossible to confide in a friend: If the friend was not familiar with Ken it would not register anyway: If the friend knew of Ken and was not receiving letters from Ken as well, it could sound like bragging. Since I am older than Ken I assumed I would go first and that would be the end of the letters. Beyond this, I had not begun to think.

After Ken passed and my shame over rejecting his simple request to visit the Foundation subsided, a thought appeared to produce a children's book on ACIM. I worked up what I thought was a beautiful tribute to Ken as well as an inspiration for children. If parents raised their children on the Course concepts they would grow up with the benefits and not have to wait years before coming to the conclusion: "there must be another way," (Schucman, 1976). This would avoid years of undoing misconceptions and give children a head-start on their spirituality.

While exploring avenues for publication I am reminded the ACIM Foundation is committed to publishing only Ken's material. *The Foundation for Inner Peace* (FIP) is mandated to publish only *A Course in Miracles* Blue book by Helen Schucman. Because I am unfamiliar with the publishing process I was looking for possible satellite divisions that may circumvent the limits of both ACIM and FIP.

After FIP asked why I thought my material would benefit children, somehow, in my effort to explain this my connection to Ken came tumbling out. Tamara asked me to provide sample letters, which I took as – **prove it!** A logical request – thus, I decided to comply.

The reaction was a huge surprise as I was encouraged to publish our letters 'because they were so beautiful!' How others should see another side of Ken besides his serious Course Lecturer persona. To say I was stunned by this revelation is an understatement! It took a while to absorb the magnitude of this evaluation. Would it be considered disrespectful to Ken to have our letters published – was my first thought!

After six years of silence should I now shout it to the world – when Ken is gone and unable to advise one way or another? What about hiding the letters and making them *special*? Is not that counter to the Course teachings - making our letters look like missals of deceit instead of Psalms of unconditional love?

Damn you, Kenneth Wapnick! You could have covered this before leaving in such a rush...

What if Ken's passing was not the rush it appeared to be to us on the outside? Cancer can take years to consume one's essence – perhaps Ken had known even before my first letter. Ken was no dummy – he was erudite, elegant, genteel and private. A book person and public figure he had to be aware of the potential of selling a single letter, or even his autograph - let alone a series of over 450 letters.

During the weeks following this revelation it occurred to me perhaps Ken expected me to publish our story for the same reason – to demonstrate how the Course works and what this means: The potential to discover unconditional love is available to everyone, not reserved for a chosen few! In addition, Ken's devotion to the Course was transparent, thus I do not believe he left behind letters contrary to his beliefs.

Reading through our letters there is this central thread of unconditional love. Sure, the letters are peppered with words of affection and silliness. It is clear how most of my letters were constantly testing Ken, and I believe his letters of affection could have been testing me, also. Ken's subtle support changed my life forever without any conscious effort on my part.

From the beginning I told Ken it was my job to make him smile, his muse – of sorts. In the process I was the one who changed because of Ken's sense of humor and support while never deviating from the Course.

First Letter to Kenneth Wapnick, Ph.D.

August 19, 2007

Dear Dr. Wapnick,

It has taken me a long time to write to you, or at least write and actually post my letter. Now that I have made up my 'mind' to communicate, I feel like I'm writing to Santa Claus; 'cause that's as close to true love as I have dared to go.

For the past three plus years I have been a facilitator for the Course, and a more unlikely person to attempt it could not have been chosen. How I talked myself into it was by thinking all I really had to do was, show up, unlock the church, turn on the lights, fan, etc. and bring water. After that, we read!

It never occurred to me that people would drop out because I was committed to sticking to the Course. It did occur to me that perhaps I should learn what the Course was about in the first place, instead of followed how the previous the facilitator had scanned the Miracles in the front of the book, read from the text while I tried to look alert.

Thinking I was a peaceful person I was shocked to see full on rage rock in, at the drop of a hat, too! There were personalities in the group that stirred red faced anger to my quiet spirit, and yet I sat liquefied in silence.

Okay! So, I don't know everything, I'm here to LEARN, and stop telling me I need to apologize to someone when we just met! I was furious, yet knew better than to respond in more than a casual acknowledgement.

The only time we met I told you I loved the Course, you took my face in both hands, kissed my cheek, and said, 'read it again!' Lately I have been listening to, A Journey from the Ego Self to the True Self and when you came to the face behind the face of innocence, I cried because I know it's true. Instead of being scared I felt as if someone had finally been honest with me.

Now, my question... The world is an illusion, a projection of our perception and over long ago. (I'm thinking this is turning into an ego question); anyway, could it be that every time we slip into our ego self we perpetuate this Illusion? Say it isn't soooooooo.

"Nice to hear from you. I am so sorry I ruined your life, and I hope you can forgive me. I also am sorry for my answer to your question. Indeed, every time we slip into our egos we perpetuate the illusion. However, we can outsmart the ego by forgiving ourselves for doing so. This way, we can have our ego's cake, and yet not have to eat it," (Wapnick, 2007).

August 27, 2007

Dear Dr. Wapnick,

I thought you might scold me for being cheeky and admitting I now love you more than

Santa Claus; instead, you apologize for ruining my life?

How can I forgive you when it isn't ruined, yet; Wait! Do you have something in 'mind'? .... and, keep in 'mind' any sleight of hand directed at me will return to you, post haste. I learned that from y-o-u...

Thank you for your prompt response to my ego question. I wasn't sure how that fit in if the world was over long ago. It's all so crazy mad that it almost makes sense. I special relationship it!

"Glad to hear your life isn't ruined - yet. But stick around a bit more and who knows what wonderful things may yet happen - even more wonderfuller than before (though not to the ego)," (Wapnick, 2007).

September 22, 2007

Dear Dr. Kenneth,

No sooner had I received your last letter than all blank let loose! It's as if you have X-ray or holographic vision, at least.

Now it looks like I have some ego management issues to work out forcing me to, of all things; FORGIVE! (Don't you hate it when you're right and still have to forgive?)

"I am so, so sorry I was right. Can you ever forgive me? Anyway, dear, keep working at it without working at it, if you know what I mean. A gentle giggle goes a long way in diffusing the ego's seriousness." (Wapnick, 2007).

October 1, 2007

Dear Doctor,

ME forgive YOU? Now, there's a concept!

In the theatre of the mind, YOU; are the Master Puppeteer; me, a papier-mâché' charwoman with tangled strings just happy to be in the box.

I rest a moment upon my sticks whilst gazing up at you with furrowed brow; a sneaky grin travels reluctantly across my lips, HARK! ..... and then I remembered, we are ONE! Works for me!

"Works for me, too; you sly one, you. But then, you don't have the fourth edition of the Course, the one with the newly-found Lesson 366, which says: The puppet and the puppeteer are one. But I think you got it anyway." (Wapnick, 2007).

This is how our letters began.

I was still trying to comprehend the ramifications of my situation, injured, out of work, and grounded for double vision (difficult enough for a professional driver), while researching options to maintain my sanity. I settled on either learning Spanish or enrolling in classes online. After three months a very persistent university counselor convinced me to register for online classes, beginning January 2008.

My thinking was online classes would at least take my focus off of my situation. Thus, advancing my education became synchromantic to my survival. It represented keeping to a schedule and giving me a purpose – both having been eliminated by the accident. Plus – I might even learn something in the process.

At the beginning I did not realize how Ken's weekly letters had become the support that kept me going, and may have influenced my decision to register in online classes, in the first place.

February 14, 2008

Dear Dr. Silly,

How cheeky of me to think I could out fox the Fox!

Only three weeks into my online academic adventure and already I'm thinking I'm Sherlock or what?

One of the things we have in common!

You had me on the edge of my chair laughing with that promise not to hurt you. Moi? How could I possibly hurt what doesn't exist, my widdo koo-ka-loo?

Worn and torn, by the indecisiveness of multiple doctors, who have marshaled me through the ranks since the accident last May: Miss, Know-it-all took matters into, what she thinks of as, her own hands. In the rainy, wet, and cold, she jumps into her new car to take care of business. Besides the guilt, which we both know doesn't exist, all went well. Mission accompli!

Second time, a few days later: again, all is well. Third time, that ol' charmer had a seizure, hits the curb and bashed the rim of the front wheel. #%@$@3%#! "Well, there you go again, smart ass!" I heard a voice say. So, I'm back to watching the grass grow and waiting for my mail!

Love, is in the Air!

"Love can be so, so boring."

(Wapnick, 2008).

Dear Ken,

By the way, I told god what you said about love being boring: when last I saw him he had a big stick and was heading your way!! How can you be the love doctor and yet think love is boring? (!. ...and, anyway; Valentine's Day has passed, so love is no longer in the air!).

I think this joke is funny and reminds me how we (I) sometimes forget who gets the credit.

A cute, young blonde is circling the block in her convertible, searching for a parking space. She is running late for her nail appointment and is very upset.

Looking up she prays, Oh God, Pleeeeze help me find a parking space, I just can't be late for my nail appointment. Pleeeeze, Pleeeeze, God! If you find me a parking space I promise I'll go to church every Sunday for the rest of my life! I promise I'll pray every day, from now on; just don't let me be late for this appointment!

As she rounds the corner, she finds a parking space, looks up and says, 'Never mind, God: I found one!

You Take My Breath Away

You take my breath away and place a song within my heart,
The *melos* seems to say we will never be apart.
You tell me time does not exist and surely this is so,
How or why I do not care I do not need to know.

You take my breath away, the child within is singing,
The tune I know is soft and slow, a song without beginnings.
I hear the beauty of your thoughts, whose words have set the music,
A tone so full of peace and grace, with love if you but choose it.

You take my breath away, the man within has risen,
With outstretched arms he lifts the child, who now is just a vision.
A man whose heart is full of love and generous of Spirit,
Who shares the song within my heart because he placed it in it!

You take my breath away, as we travel on together,
We share Spirit and our song and journey up the ladder.
Spirit now, our song is sung: we made it home where we are One,
He kept his promise to His Son, you take my breath away!

"Thanks for your lovely poem, Bunny. I am deeply grateful.
Now it is you who take my breath away." (Wapnick, 2008).

March 07, 2008

Dear Dr. Wapnick,

It is curious to me how the poem came about. I left your letter on the table beside my computer. Returning later, as I picked it up a jolt went through me, like an electrical shock, and took my breath away. Hence, the poem. I thought it might be the HS. (?) Or, a second chance to make a first impression, or, a Holy Instant with a kick?

If you are telling me that it was you doing that, I think I may be ready for the 'Funny Farm!' Besides, although I have read it a hundred times I am unable to memorize it beyond the first verse. How silly is that!

I'm leaving, now.

"Thanks again for your lovely poem. And I like the electric jolt thing, not to mention the kicked holy instant. You is one helluva power woman. Remind me always to stay on your good side." (Wapnick, 2008).

In the beginning I suspected Ken had no idea to whom he was writing. After he appeared in spirit I gave up on trying to figure out what he knew or how he managed to transport his essence into my mind. I believe he saw me only as a "Son of God" not a body, while I was trying to understand from the body. Did I understand what I was saying? Not for a minute!

April 12, 2008

Dear Ken,

Like a phoenix we ascended the mist into a darkened sky. Morning sat on the horizon unpacking her rays. One by one she hung yellow across the skyline, their edges glistened like a million bees-wings flying into a sunset. We flew through the crack between night and morning as a blue sky unfolded to engulf our jet. I opened my book to catch up on a new story when the wings dipped and my heart tumbled. Surprisingly free of fear I returned to my book without looking up.

The smiling face of one beloved daughter greeted me upon my arrival. She loaded my luggage into her car and we embarked on the hour drive to Tucson. Like two squirrels sharing stories of our buried pantry we chatted the hour away. I have yet to tell her that we are one because on some level she already knows it to be so: a sure case of daughter having been born before her mother.

We joined the wedding party for our scheduled massages, returning to the lobby like a group of wet socks. Filled with oils and a dash of euphoria, I looked at least half an hour younger. It's too bad one cannot bottle giggles 'cause my family was blessed with the giggle gene. I tried coca cola with peanuts, as recommended by the groom's fellow Marine friend and decided whoever thought that one up must have been high on moonshine.

Back to the compound to unpack, street fair, church for final touches, rehearsal dinner, bed. Who can sleep, it's fresh and warm and there is a lot of catching up to do. Wide eyed and jabber jawed I camped out on granddaughters bed catching up with her journey. A late nite trip to Circle K for a pint of milk that I should have smeared on my face, but it tastes soooo good I had to drink it. Morning rang, family took over street fair, last minute shopping, and dressing for the big event.

A 5' 9" masterpiece of a granddaughter walked down the aisle on the arm of her daddy, looking like the top piece on a fantasy wedding cake. If beauty were a measure of one's worth, she would be priceless. Truth is, she is beautiful inside and out. Here's when it's good to remember we are all one! (Yeah, yeah, I know; it doesn't work like that). On the arm of her handsome groom, in his dress blues; they climbed aboard a glass Cinderella carriage, drawn by silver horses. Looking for-all-the-world like Princess Diana in her coach, they rode to the reception. If I could only dance like that every night I would be at least an inch taller.

By the following evening I was riding home with a cranky cab driver. Whatever. Sometimes it is harder than other times to picture how we are all one... faith, I say.. .and all of this between your letters.

My best news is, no more seizures!! Three CT scans didn't find it, an MRI didn't find it, only my physical therapist found it. The first cervical rib on my left side, up by my neck, was out of the socket!! For 11 months I have been telling the doctors that it feels like a stick is stabbing me and they just looked at me with eyes glazed over.

Although it was screamingly painful to be shoved into place, I felt the blood rushing into my arm and hand and knew that was what was casing my hand to go to sleep. I felt so much better it took me a couple of days to realize I was also seizure free!!

It's good to know I'm not crazy, even though I am scheduled to see a psychiatrist next week. For a head injury?! And, this little toe cried, ha, ha, ha, all the way home!

The next block of classes started last Monday and I will now be learning how to critically think! While I ponder the problem that you think you are thinking.

"I love the way you write, my dear friend: warm, literate, and personal, without being schlurpy, (Wapnick, 2008).

Dear Ken,

On the premise we are One; I take you with me everywhere I go, in my mind, I will admit only to being your muse, a 'lovely' (I like that) menchy- muse. And you, Dear Dr. Silly, are my 'quirky' Koo-ka-loo. (See? I'm still listening to, The Decision Maker!) Your nice words are honey on my peanut butter but, schlurpy's live over there in 7-11.

Having a passion for opera, did you ever go to the brown-bag operas'? I am just guessing San Francisco stole the idea from New York and wondered if you used to go brown-bagging? Heaven forbid you move or rattle your bag lunch else someone smacks you over the head with their sheet music. It still makes me laugh. Now, those were the good old days, yeah! (Holographic, of course).

(Ken had never heard of a Brown-Bag-Opera so I explained):

Brown-bag Opera

The San Francisco Opera House had a lunchtime program, called, Brown-bag Opera. You could bring a bag lunch and listen to the opera rehearse. In fact, the Opera House used to sell bag lunches. There were no sets, costumes, or scenery; only full cast and music. The crowds were more intimate making it easy to engage in conversation with members of the cast.

Devotees brought their sheet music and had convulsions if one made any noise. I often took a cable car to the Opera House and occasionally brought a client with me. Long lunch hours were one of the perks for being a Trust Officer. I still have fond memories of the experience.

Thoughts:

Sometimes things happen that cannot be explained. When this occurs it must mean it was meant to be! It feels like my whole life has been a struggle. Often fun, or interesting, but always one step ahead of me! Still, it is not in my nature to give up! In fact, my motto has always been, when one door slams shut, look for a window to open. Most of the events in my life before Ken did not alert me to what was about to take place. In the future if someone wishes to communicate with me there are easier ways than waiting until I have a broken neck.

2

My Big-Bang!

How a Broken Neck led me to Kenneth Wapnick, Ph.D.

*T*he real reason for writing that first letter to Kenneth Wapnick, Ph.D. remains a bit of a mystery. In the total scheme of things, it is unacceptable to write a non-professional letter to a professional for any reason. To take over a page of nonsense to ask one question is unheard of, yet that is the way our correspondence began. Once he answered my question I had no idea he would continue to write. With each letter I figured it would be the last time I ever heard from him! Whatever the reason, my first letter led us on an odyssey covering the next six years when Ken passed.

Just three months prior to the letter my vehicle was struck by a City bus running a red light, breaking my neck, and ending my career, income, and social life all in one little instant, (I call it my Big-Bang!). I continue to bring the accident into the scenario because as tragic as it was for me the fact I survived at all is a gift (same intersection five days later a bus ran the same light, struck and killed the woman).

In addition, I am no longer the person I was before the accident and now I am all alone to ponder. My future was in limbo, a situation not penciled in during the few times I thought about retirement. In one of Ken's letters he claims he did not send the bus, however it did slow me down so he could catch up with me! This comment is a total role reversal statement and some sort of paradox. I am the one in awe of our connection and Ken suggests he was waiting for me? Thus, if not for the accident none of this would have taken place!

December 30, 2007

Dear Ken,

What I find especially endearing about you is the loving, genteel way you edit my messages... and, yes, I am silly/playful and I'm too old to change, so there! Sometimes I can be as serious as a heart attack only to discover things didn't become better because I became serious-er. (O b quiet)

When I was born you were still in God's pocket. I now realize having reached critical mass ahead of you did not necessarily give me a head start. It took me over 60 years to find you AND YOU'RE NOT GETTING AWAY NOW! so, get used to silly.

There is a reason why I am telling you what I am about to tell you and there is a reason why I didn't tell you before. I am telling you because you addressed the issue on an old tape and I have an ACIM question following.

The reason I didn't tell you before was because I respect your professional expertise and would not expect professional advice without doing the proper channels stuff. In fact, I'm cheeky enough to think I don't even need professional help, just the affection of a professional person will do just fine.

Photo of vehicle

So, on May 19, 2007 1 was struck by a City bus running a red light and that's the reason I was looking for a PI Attorney. On your tape, ego self to True Self you mention a person having been struck by a vehicle running a red light. It's an old tape and I'm sure it was recorded before my accident, yet it spoke to me. Are you saying we/1 may have caused the accident on some level? And if so, where's my Jaguar?

Bottom line, I look normal. The configuration of my head has changed and I now have new bumps and dents. Plus, concussion, double-vision and seizures, but they don't hurt. What hurts is I'm not allowed to drive, ANYTHING or ANYWHERE!!!
 I knew one day I would be put out to pasture I just thought it would be a gradual thing. What I didn't know is the pasture is full of old heifers! I miss driving, having a routine and most of all, I miss having a purpose.

"And as for the accident, you - Bunny - had nothing to do with it. But you - the decision maker - of course is dreaming it. But the worst thing you can do with a situation is metaphysicalize it (I channeled that word). But, what you can do is be peaceful midst this horror show. Let's keep this simple, especially since Jesus hates complicated. How and why something happened is irrelevant once it happened, but your reaction to it is the key. So, my dear silly friend, giggle at the silliness of the situation, and smile your way home, even as you graze in the pasture with the heifers." (Wapnick, 2008).

Results of an Accidental Connection

My first reaction was one of disbelief as I learned the bus company blamed me for the accident! They claimed I ran the red light and struck the bus head-on! What about the fact the bus was traveling north on a busy seven lane **one-way boulevard** while I was on a cross street! They went on to claim nearly

$40,000 damage to the rear of the bus and it was not the same bus number as the bus listed on the police report.

There are numerous things wrong with this: 1) Do you actually believe I would attempt to run a red light and cross seven-lanes of a busy one-way boulevard with a passenger in my vehicle - seriously! 2) It is impossible to strike anything head-on on a seven lane one-way boulevard coming from a cross street – not even if you have a death wish, which I do not! 3) On the off-chance I actually managed to strike the bus head-on how come the damage was only to the rear of the bus, and why am I still here? 4) Never mind the bus claiming the damage was not the same bus number as listed on the police report!

By the time the truth of what happened to my case was revealed my online studies in Criminal Justice were addressing organized crime. How after Prohibition officially ended it took government 20 years to realized (admit?) organized crime had gone underground by investing in legal businesses where they could laundry their money unnoticed. I'm just saying!

The irony – my license was suspended because of double-vision forcing me to ride the very monsters who caused the accident! Every ride I am witnessing the bus driver running red lights. When I inquired why this was so each driver had the same answer: They are required to because they have a schedule to meet! Plus, that is why the bus stops are on the other side of the intersection! This is not a secret within the industry and bus drivers will tell you this if you ask.

Included in this wealth of information – bus companies enjoy the uninsured status, meaning: bus companies do not carry insurance – in the event of an accident they hire a company to 'mop-up' and send them a bill. This is not unusual within the transportation industry and it is more cost effective than carrying insurance. The caveat is any company using this system must be bonded and demonstrate their ability to pay in the event of an accident.

After learning this in class and putting it together with my case I realized this is why my attorney dropped my case and why I wrote to Ken regarding an honest PI attorney. Attorneys can hold out for recognition from the transportation company and settle out of court. Likely why my attorney had not filed a claim during the five months he had my case.

When I learned my attorney had not filed a claim but I still had 29 days to do so, I filed the claim with the City. It took five months for the City to respond with an excuse the City has no jurisdiction over the bus company; and I must file directly with the bus company. Unfortunately, the six-month period to file with the bus had passed and the negotiations were over.

On-the-other-hand I believe things turn out the way they were meant to. Besides, to expect me to take care of business and fight for what is right makes sense until one realizes I had a **broken neck** (it took doctors 11 months to discover and admit – by then it had healed crooked – Atlas Subluxation). Now, I must sleep propped-up. If I slip off my stack of pillows I am unable to get up unless I lift my head with both hands. This is not normal.

My seizures were totally unpredictable: loss of concentration, no multitasking! Double-vision, (Diplopia) which complicates things but is not painful unless my eye starts to spin: in addition to dealing with these issues as a senior citizen, alone. As usual, I tried to move on and deal with it by overlooking what should have been, (total denial of my situation).

The results of my ineffective way of dealing with the legal issues, along with a collection of incompetent medical professionals, led me to Ken... Since we were already corresponding when my attorney dropped my case it made sense to ask Ken for a referral: otherwise, I would not have bothered him with issues outside the Course.

Thoughts:

If anyone had told me my career would end with a broken neck I would have said something inspirational like, "Thanks a Lot!" Three weeks after the accident I turned 71. While I should have had a plan for retirement, I had basically shelved any thoughts on the subject. In the back of my mind I did not 'see' myself as that old, thus no need to think on it, yet. The universe had other ideas.

A good example of how things turn out the way they were meant to be.

3

Chalk & Cheese

The Sophisticate and the Char-Woman Puppet

In the theater of the mind, You – are the Master Puppeteer: me? a paper-mache` charwoman with tangled strings, just happy to be in the box. I rest a moment upon my sticks whilst gazing up at you with furrowed brow. A sneaky grin travels reluctantly across my lips. HARK! Then I remembered, we are One, (My Mantra).

The beloved teacher of *A Course in Miracles*, Dr. Wapnick was a dedicated and serious lecturer. Dr. Wapnick spoke multiple languages, wrote many books, posted his YouTube lectures, and published the Lighthouse quarterly newsletter. As a quiet man with a private persona; opera, classical music, Shakespeare, and Freud, were tops on his list.

In contrast, I grew up in foster care from the age of three and placed in a church school where we were taught our God was the real God. By the age of eight I was asking questions such as, "How many God's are up there, anyway? Our God (the real God), the Jewish God, African God, Catholic God, Chinese God, How many?" Eyes rolled, yet no answers came forth. This same quirkiness can be seen in my letters and may be responsible for bringing out the silly side of Ken seldom seen. If my comments were silly, Ken's response was equally silly. If I joked with him he had a quick retort just as funny, only subtle. When he expressed affection it was followed by something silly. He never asked questions and when I asked if he knew of an *honest* Personal Injury Attorney he referred me to his attorney never questioning why I had asked. It took two more months before it occurred to me I may not have thanked him properly or explained. I did this by sending photos of my vehicle after the crash. He responded by telling me I made his day! (A simple act of sharing made his day!). Who is this guy, anyway?

As the weeks, then months passed I occasionally encouraged Ken to talk about his earlier years, however he never opened up about his personal life. Perhaps because what he wanted known was already in print, and if I really cared I could look it up. Could also be by asking about his past would have required placing him back into his body, when in fact he had transcended his body long before, plus, the past is past!

Ken had a playful side and skillfully adjusted my spelling, grammar, and typos. Although good with all three I was now working with seizures, double-vision causing letters to 'swim,' loss of memory (out of sight-out of mind), and loss of concentration (no multitasking)! He never mentioned my errors, instead responded using the same word in corrected form in his next letter. Even if I asked he never acknowledged his corrections. By the third month we were using first names – equals!

In the letter where Ken tells me I had made it to *The Little Garden* (T-18, VIII) he was not making up something just for me. I had gone beyond the point of no return. I now understood the difference between the ego and unconditional love and furthermore, had the tools to immediately correct myself and move on – not become stuck or overwhelmed by guilt.

After he told me I had made it to the end of an ancient journey I cried like a baby because part of this beautiful passage spoke to me: "Yet He Whom you welcomed has come to you, and would welcome you. He has waited long to give you this. Receive it now of Him, for He would have you know Him." (T-18, VIII-13:1-8).

Another beautiful aspect of our letters is Ken never preaches his beliefs, he may remind me of the silliness of the dream without quoting segments from the Course, unless I asked. Eventually I understood just from his steadfast and unmovable kindness in spite of my quirkiness (constant testing).

In retrospect, during the first two-plus years especially, I went to doctors three times a week trying to identify and treat the effects of the accident. It took five months for a hematoma larger than my hand, on top of my head, to dissipate. If I put any pressure on the left side of my face it felt mushy and my left eye was spinning. This took over four years to subside and what I learned later was swelling on the left side of my head. In addition, it was 11 months later when I went to a different doctor and learned not only had my neck been broken and healed crooked, my first cervical rib was out-of-socket causing seizures. I now have osteoarthritis in the left side of my face/ jaw, and eye socket. (never heard of this before).

I knew just enough about the Course not to focus on my injuries and make them real, and not to dwell on the past – which does not exist – or complain about my situation (injured - out of work - homeless) and deny the Course while writing to Kenneth Wapnick, Ph.D. ACIM Master Lecturer! (explains why my letters tend to be silly stuff).

Ken understood he was not a body and lived it. I accepted the concept we are a mind in a body, (classroom) not a body with a mind because the idea has been around for a long time. However, when Ken appeared to me while sleeping and confirmed it in his next letter it was like – wait a minute! If this really happened there is something more going on here! Ever slammed on the brakes when you discover you are heading in the wrong direction – than making a quick U-turn – in the middle of the street? That was my U-turn moment!

After Ken confirmed his visit and spoke of meeting again, I could not wait for his next visit. This was exciting on at least two levels: First, that Ken could somehow project himself into my mind making a virtual appearance, and secondly, somehow I had channeled Ken! I surged with energy! For a short period of time I did silly things, such as, stop by my bed or ottoman (holy-moly), sit down, close my eyes, and say something profound like, "Okay Ken, where are you?" It did not work this way – Ken's visits came during the night when I was relaxed and not thinking about visits from Ken.

Ken's First Visit

May 13, 2008

Dear Ken,

Okay, last night I made up my mind to go to bed early, only because I wanted to get up early, leave the apartment early, and run my errands, before I settled down to my homework.

At 10:30 p.m. I turned out the lights, television, locked the doors, and went down for the night. I awoke around 1:30 a.m. and was not in the mood to return to sleep. I wasn't sad, tired, stressed or any other reason I could think of. Perhaps it was too warm upstairs, I really cannot say.

I went downstairs, turned on some music and curled up on the ottoman to listen. The room was dark except for a faint glow from the lights in the courtyard outside. How much time elapsed, I am not sure; but I fell back asleep and the most beautiful feeling overcame me.

It seemed like I was awake, or awaken by the presence of a person standing beside me. I remember being embarrassed for having been caught asleep on the ottoman, until the person spoke. I am not certain I actually heard any words, yet such a tender feeling came over me that it put me immediately at ease.

In the darkness I did not focus on the face, just the silhouette of this person, still: the essence was as if you were standing beside me. There was nothing physical about it, just a reassurance that all was going to work out. It seemed so normal it never occurred to me to be afraid, or worried, or even surprised!

I continued to bathe in the aftermath of pleasures glow before opening my eyes to the thinnest of the dark. I felt caressed, and loved. It no longer mattered if you were there in form or Spirit, you left your love behind.

Turning on the lamp, I picked up the ACIM manual, it opened to: I am as God created me. The feeling of peace has been with me ever since.

"Thanks again for letting me come, for letting me stay, and for sharing the tender love with me." (Wapnick, 2008).

The following is my letter to Ken after he confirms his first visit.

May 25, 2008

Dear Ken,

Your recent photovoltaic message is still smoldering in my mind. You completely decoded my well placed defenses with your confirmation. It's a beautiful thing.

My pathetic attempt to respond fell far short of what was dwelling within my mind. Things were passing by so fast it felt like I was surfing on a stream of white light. I could still see, feel and hear, but I had no idea how to absorb the impact of your message.

A lifelong desire to have a relationship like ours was being played out before me, and within me. The silence of your tender words resonated throughout my being. I will forever wear them carved upon my heart.

(Author's note January 2016).

As I write this I can still feel the bouquet of emotions from our first meeting. How could I be dreaming when Ken confirmed his visit? People do not confirm appearing in ones dreams! Since he has confirmed it how do I now explain it? If I try to explain our connection at least two things are guaranteed to happen. I will look like a fool because of who Ken was. Plus, it could tend to place a question about my credibility.

Not because Ken lacked the potential to travel in spirit, in fact – if anyone could do so, Ken would be the first person to come to mind. However, who the hell do I think I am to claim he appeared to me? Explain that! While you are at it, explain how Ken left behind such a feeling of peace and love! (You cannot make this up!).

Only after Ken's passing and my opportunity to relocate did I realize the full impact of our connection. "When spirit's original state of direct communication is reached, neither the body nor the miracle serves any purpose" (T-1, V-1:2). While this verifies the ability to communicate in spirit exists, it does not address the emotions, the Peace, and Unconditional Love Ken always left behind.

"No one in my long and boring life has ever met me on the holy-moly."

(Wapnick, 2008).

Now, is Ken saying I am the only one who has acknowledged his out-of-body visits – or could he be saying of his usual out-of-body visits I am the only one with a holy-moly? To me, either way this could be taken it is still another Gift.

Although I referred to our visits as out-of-body Ken never gave it a name and ignored my requests to explain. Makes sense now, knowing it was not something Ken would say – Yep, that was me – Dontcha love it?! He simply waited for me to get it, and sorry to say he had passed before the truth became clear to me.

No, I am not there, yet!

Did I say I never had trouble with the 2 + 2 = 5 concept or rode the fence occasionally – no. I am admitting having trouble verbally expressing unconditional love on paper because it looks so similar to expressing ego based love in any form. Besides, how do you express in the illusion what is not of the ego? Remember, my background did not include love or affection and I had already warned Ken about my confusion. In addition, if his letters included expressions of affection they were usually signed by a staff member. Ken, never deviated from the Course – another Gift from Ken.

Without Ken's letters confirming his visits it would have been difficult believing it myself or convincing anyone of Ken's visits. While to some it may sound like a love story, it is not. Rather, I like to think of it as a story of Love, a concept which seldom came up in my vernacular while growing up.

Then again, according to the Course when we are in our right mind where all are one, we do experience the total love of God. On that concept, it is a normal state of mind when out of the ego. Now, I Love that!

July 18, 2008

You bring me joy!

Each morning after my shower, I listen to at least one of your CD's while I perform magic on my face and hair. Currently, I am listening to the Decision Maker, again. I love your essence, the way you interact with your audience, and your passion for the Course. Sometimes I even hear you breathe. Why this is fun for me is, I just realized I never fell in love with Ken, the body, in the first place. That was never my focus. Okay, perhaps I had an occasional ego moment over your dimple, but you became a part of me and my thoughts a long time ago.

I love that you are the intellectual, the sophisticated one, my spirit guide, if there is such a thing. I know I'm a 'piece of work,' the charwoman puppet, leaning on her sticks, gazing up at the Master Puppeteer. But, I'm lovable, and lucky for me, it is too late for you to return to pre-Bunz. (so say I)

There is something peaceful about a spiritual love affair. For one thing, you are always there for me, and occasionally I feel your presence. The concept takes some getting used to, it's a little out there, but out there is where I have always been, anyway.

So, my Koo-ka-loo, I would never think of giving up a spiritual love affair. Occasionally, I do feel so close to you I find myself wanting to touch you, but that must be my bad ass ego?! (Ken's response is priceless!).

"And how so very cool that you - you lovable one, bad ass ego and all – love my dimples (but why do you only love one when your Koo-ka-loo has two!)." (Wapnick, 2008).

August 22, 2008

Dear Est kid,

You-so-silly. I'll just steal the book out of the church library.

Else, how will I know if you have two dimples if you do not send a photo?

Everyone has heard of Freud, but what I knew about him I pretty much learned from your CD's. Left to select the topic for our essay, it popped into my head to do Freud. In the process, I had the opportunity to see who he was as, the man.

I enjoyed the process, earned a good grade, and decided to leave Freud and his psychoanalytical insights up to the master...you.

What I'm really saying is I don't want you to know what an amateur I am, yet.

Love

Dear Ken,

The love I am feeling is only a rational expression of any quadratic formula solved by simply identifying a, b, and c, and inserting the coefficient to correspond with the x-intercepts, the one rational solution.

Your ode to rain has not been glanced over, and who cares what it means when the true identity has applied itself with a soft-spoken notion? A visit on your birthday night could only have been you. That silent rocking turned my head as I waited expectantly for you to appear. It worked as an affirmation to complete my algebra, and today's grades reflected the value of that decision, a solid 97 percent. Had I navigated the radical sign it would have been 100 percent. To maintain the trend for this week and next week will guarantee that I have successfully passed Algebra II. (Thank you for sending White Light).

"You are such a love, a dear love. Your ever-loving Koo-Ka-Loo really appreciates you. Ah, that first letter! What a come on. So nicely set up by our Holy-Moly, stinging thumb and all. Keep nudging me about a poem." (Wapnick, 2011).

January 20, 2011

My Dearest Ken,

Last night---my hand felt your warmth, and it was not the cat sitting on my bed!

These events remind me that I/we are not alone, (poem) just when I need it most. Why I seem compelled to (poem) relate these events to you, when you are so far ahead of me, could only mean I am lost in my attempt to show respect, while broadcasting my glee (poem) over our connection! You already know that? (p~o~e~m).

I am loving my new class, Ethics in Criminal Justice. What?! No such thing... (poem) Anyway, this is the (poem) first week, and no grade on the last (poem) class, yet. Last report, meaning up to week four, of a five week (poem) class, my grade was 97.7%. So, I am not worried about passing, as long as I maintain (poem) a decent grade.

This quote caught my attention:

By Maj. Gen Jerry E. White, USAFR

"We have grasped the mystery of the atom and rejected the Sermon on the Mount. The world has achieved brilliance without wisdom, power without conscience. Ours is a world of nuclear giants and ethical infants."

My Dearest, I accept the concept of past, present, and future (poem) being the same, please stay with me until it is possible for me to live it. Thank you for bringing me back when I slip, and for nudging me when I mention (poem) something from before that is no longer relevant.

Reflections

Over the years I became comfortable with Ken's 'out-of-body' visits – it was not unusual to feel his weight sitting on the edge of my bed. Often, I could see the indentation in my covers while the body remained invisible. If I held out my hand asking him to hold it – I could feel the pressure as he complied with my request. It reminded me of the movie Ghost – again, Ken allowed me to ramble on without correcting me, or explaining.

Recently, shortly after I turned out the lights, I felt pressure on the side of my bed. In addition, I felt the covers near my upper body pulled in the direction of the pressure, meaning something heavy had just landed. I raised my head and said, "That better be you, Ken because I no longer have a kitty!" Almost immediately, I fell fast asleep...

These visits were in addition to communicating in spirit and at first I needed proof for my sanity – until I realized - I am living it and it has been confirmed, so what more do I need. Can I explain it? No, but I accept it because it was Ken. This is why it is still embarrassing for me to admit how I told Ken he would not know who I was if I visited the Foundation.

Not only would he have known who I was, this recent visit not only came since his passing, but he was too ill to respond to my letter advising him I had moved to Las Vegas! And still he found me! (?). If Ken could find me with all the moving around I did during the nearly four years while homeless, he most likely would recognize me if I had visited the Foundation. I pray he has forgiven me for having been so insensitive? See, I am still trying to explain it as a body, when I should just accept it as proof we are one in spirit.

Thoughts:

I have always been the type who needs the 'facts!' I do not want to listen to a bunch of suppositions. Just tell me the truth and I will deal with it. Any attempt to convince me I was communicating in spirit better have an exceptionally creative proof-package to confirm it. So, what makes this different? Ken confirmed it in his following letter.

Yes, I have had a lot of goofy dreams over the years, about a variety of people, places and things. But, I have never had a figure from a dream write and confirm communicating with me in the dream! Not to mention leaving behind such feelings of love and peace. This is scary wonderful!

4

ACIM ~ Baggins & Fogg Books

"I am not a body. I am free. For I am as God created me."
(Lesson 199).

$\mathcal{T}$he same year *A Course in Miracles* was first published (1976) I bought a bookstore in San Francisco, because it was for sale and I love to read. The outgoing owners agreed to stay around to educate me on how to operate the business. I appreciated this since I did not have a background in owning a bookstore.

My previous employment had been the Accounting Department of a San Francisco brokerage firm, a Modeling Agency, before becoming a Trust Officer with a bank in San Francisco. I was a voracious reader and never far away from a book. The kind of person who reads walking down the street, in markets, shopping, and in the cafeteria at the bank. I bought the bookstore thinking it was a perfect match for someone who loves to read.

The reality, there was so much promotional reading required to operate the bookstore I seldom had a chance to read my preferred material. After 11 months the gift shop next door went out of business and the landlord allowed me to open an archway and expand to a total 3,100 (sf). The building was old and charming with chandeliers, carpets, plants, antiques, and two kitties, Shiloh and Pooky. It was an exciting time in my life and I enjoyed every minute.

One morning a young lady came in asking for the book, *A Course in Miracles*, (ACIM). It did not stand out in my memory, although I had a few books on miracles. Nonetheless, I led her to the section on New Age Religions to search and discovered I actually had one copy of ACIM!

As I rang up her purchase she clutched the book to her chest and exclaimed how she loved the book and how it had changed her life forever! She looked so happy! Her enthusiasm was infectious! For a moment I felt a tinge of regret that I was not experiencing such elation. I promptly ordered a replacement of ACIM, and made a mental note to look into the book when it arrived in a couple of days.

When the replacement arrived I skimmed through, saw words like 'God this and God that, and decided it was just another religious book and returned it to the shelf. For several days, thoughts of our conversation lingered just behind my consciousness while I went about my business. One day I must look into the book, *A Course in Miracles*, and see if it would affect my life in some profound way.

In 1966 my only son was killed in a hit-and-run. He and a friend wanted to walk home the back road which was a short distance from a church picnic at the Country Club. With my four girls inside the car and the boys riding on the trunk, I drove slowly to the top of the hill to meet up with the back road. The two boys started off down the road, and then my son came back saying, "I forgot to kiss my mama Good-bye!" That was to be the last time I saw him alive. (How to explain that?).

By the time I drove home with my four daughters the phone was ringing and I learned my son was in the hospital. In those days the emergency room would not allow relatives in with the patients, not even the mother – thus, I never saw my son again until the night before his funeral, three days later. He would have turned 12 in less than two months. I did not go to church, or church functions again for 30 years!

More years passed, now a Chauffeur in Southern California I drove a famous Grammy Award Gospel singer who also was the pastor of a church. His music was so beautiful and inspiring I started attending his church – for two and a half years! One Sunday as I approached the church one of his Aides told me where to find a nice White church just down the road a few miles. I was shocked!

In January 2003 I was fired from the Limousine Company for taking my screenplay to a studio on my day off! This did not compute – since when does your employer have jurisdiction over one's day off? In their effort to explain they claimed I also tried to sell my script to a passenger, however the passenger referenced was returning from a skiing trip and slept all the way home. Besides, it was not something I would do. However, I was the oldest female driver and the two next to oldest women drivers were already on disability. (Bingo!).

Somewhere, in the following weeks I went to Barnes & Noble, sat in on a book reading, and met two women looking for a purpose. We began exploring our options, Buddhism, Kabbalah, Tapping classes, Edgar Cayce classes, Meditation, Metaphysical sessions, Drum Circles, and last - *A Course in Miracles*! I had almost forgotten about it.

Eventually, in 2003 I went back to driving for another limo company, while attending ACIM at Unity Church. Shortly thereafter, the facilitator transferred out of state leaving me in charge. It could have been terrifying because I did not understand all of it: yet, I was pleased the facilitator thought enough of me to leave me in charge.

After the accident I had more time to concentrate on the text, listen to Ken's CD's, and watch his YouTubes. By now, I had become hooked on the Course. Not to mention I happened to write to Ken in 2007 for clarification on a concept (referenced earlier) beginning our weekly communication over the next six years. This process, and through Ken's loving support, I believe my understanding of the Course was fast-forwarded collapsing time needed to understand.

Ken began joining with me in spirit in May 2008 and continued these visits on a regular basis until he passed in December 2013. Although I was humbled by the magnitude of unconditional love and peace he always left behind, I still did not realize the full impact on my life – until Ken passed. For example, I thought Ken was appearing in my dreams – whereas, I have mentioned this before Ken never mentioned I too must lapse into spirit in order to meet with Ken in spirit – Nor did I understand Ken was building a foundation of unconditional love with his constant support.

This must be so because now I do not seem to feel threatened when I catch myself in my ego: I just forgive myself and move on. "I am not a body. I am Free. For I am as God created me." I accept unconditional love comes from a Higher Power, and is available whether I recognize it or not. I can ignore it, but I cannot destroy it.

It explains why he told me I do not need to go to ACIM classes, I had made it to the Little Garden and once there you do not go back – just live it. Not until Ken was gone and I began reading our letters did I realize I finally understood what the young lady in my bookstore meant when she said ACIM had changed her life forever. My life had also been changed forever – by concepts from the book, *A Course in Miracles* – and mostly with Ken's love and support.

"Of course you don't go back. From where would you be going, never having been there in the first place? Silly!" (Wapnick 2009).

Thoughts:

Although it took six years of letters from Ken to convince me I was actually joining him in spirit, I believe I had accepted the concept much earlier. Certain things just need time to absorb and assimilate before the concept becomes acceptable. On the one-hand the experience seemed real, but how so? On the other-hand, it came from Ken so it must be so.

Ken never explained his visits, which would have sated my need for proof. Because he never explained his visits he taught me to have faith in myself. I consider this a fair trade off.

5

A Course in Miracles - OBE & NDE

Out of Body Experience (OBE) vs. Near Death Experience (NDE)

*I*t has always been curious to me why society accepts reports of 'out-of-body' (OBE) or 'near death' (NDE) experiences: and makes movies and books about these experiences: Yet casts a jaundice eye on two healthy individuals reporting their accounts of communicating in spirit. Spirit is Spirit and available whether one is at deaths door or has accepted the concept of spiritual communication through practice and use.

Societies acceptance would add credibility to my reports of meeting with Ken, in spirit: while supporting Ken's ability to communicate in spirit. Actually, just because society has delayed accepting the concept should not mean the ability does not exist. We already know it exists, it is the application that appears to be in question.

Nonetheless, the following takes a look at what has become acceptable –NDE and OBE, (Williams, n. d.). Over the past 20 years or so we have experienced more reports of Near Death

Experiences (NDE) than ever before. There is some debate whether this is because of an increase of NDE reporting, or because advanced technology has exposed the population to more information and people are opening their minds and paying attention, or perhaps both.

After all, we now live in an age where we can communicate instantly through social media and compare our findings with individuals around the globe. When something unusual occurs whether it be NDE or OBE, or UFO's with a short 'click' the news in posted globally. So, what is the difference if two or more healthy individuals learn to communicate in spirit?

Near Death Experience, (NDE).

Reports of NDE experience differ from OBE because the individual involved has the ability to communicate with another entity from the 'other-side.' They communicate their decision to return to earth (body) or stay in the unknown, called Heaven. According to reports, Heaven is peaceful, the surroundings are vivid in color, however the most profound feeling is one of total Love! This feeling of total love is so beautiful the individual never forgets the experience once returning to this life, where they tell their stories and write books about their experience.

This is similar to my experiences when meeting Ken in spirit. The surroundings are in vivid colors and I am engulfed in total love, although not of the body - in addition I do not have to be at death's door to experience it. Why would I not want to share this experience with others when it is available to everyone?

Since I have experienced (OBE) and not (NDE) I am curious about the differences:

1) What determines whether it is possible to experience (OBE), where there is no apparent control, or (NDE), where the individual makes a choice to return?
2) Is it the magnitude of the injury that allows the patient to experience NDE?

Out-of-Body Experience, (OBE).

According to accounts, during OBE the individual does not make a departure: rather hovers overhead and observes what is taking place. Such as, after surgery the patient has awaken and is able to give a full accounting of the details of the surgery because they were hovering overhead watching.

Personally, as a teenager I was involved in a head-on collision where I went into the windshield and landed in a ditch. I have no recollection of how I made it to the hospital. Even today, I have a vivid recollection of hovering above myself while my boyfriend and his brother stood around the table where I lay unconscious. I was wearing a turquoise and white striped tunic and concerned because the pin holding the plunging neckline closed had been removed for x-rays. As a shy person it was embarrassing to me even from the ceiling. After all these years, I can still see myself on the table with my tunic open and my boyfriend and his brother watching. I remember saying, "close her top!"

At the time, it seemed normal to me…because I have always had weird sightings and experiences. Trying to relate or defining these experiences creates issues with family and friends because they tend to think you are making it up. The following website gives important information on these topics.

Out-of-Body Experiences and the Near-Death Experience

www.near-death.com/science/research/out-of-body-experiences.html

After reading current articles on OBE all patients reporting OBE were dead and came back, either naturally, or by medical recitation. Now, I wonder if I too had died and came back? The doctor did not explain this to me, and maybe he was not aware of it. To read this after so many years is enlightening, to say the least. Because of my background, if the doctor had confirmed I had died for any period of time, I would have denied the information as nonsense and given it no further thought. (My usual way of dealing with major issues-just keep going).

My hope is people will become more interested in exploring their spirituality and discover their potential to communicate while still in the body. The results could be an increase in taking better care of each other and perhaps less conflict globally. Just one experience communicating in spirit is enough to awaken an interest in developing a better understanding of the process.

Our country is in distress: the newer generations do not believe in the traditions of our past and are searching for something concrete. Eventually, maybe someone from the new generation will figure it out.

ACIM – NDE - OBE:

In the total scheme of things and in the concept we are one in spirit there must be a connection. This has to do with what Einstein called levels of energy. OBE hovers locally: the mind hovers above the body, watching and remembering. NDE travels to another dimension and communicates with another entity, probably a higher self: and ACIM is fluid and without boundaries. Ken did say we would meet again when his schedule settled down. This must mean it takes some concentration, like meditation, in preparation to communicate in spirit.

While communicating in spirit is available to everyone, there must be a transmitter and a receiver: Ken transmitted and I received. I have not been able to transmit into another's mind since Ken left. If I concentrate he will appear in spirit, not the same as initiating the communication.

It would be interesting to explore the travel itinerary of the mind to understand how the process of communicating outside the body works. Einstein suggests it is more a transfer of thought, than actually moving the body. If so, this coincides with ACIM and the idea the body is nothing, we are a Mind.

Although Ken officially passed December 27, 2013 he made an early morning visit the night before. As I lay sleeping in the shadows he took my face in both hands and kissed me on the lips, waking me. I yelled, "Stop that!" Then giggled as I realized it was Ken and begged him to return. However, Ken was on a fast track to Eternity... he left behind a room full of Peace and Unconditional Love.

Thoughts:

As someone who believes in UFO's - the concepts of Einstein's Theory along with A Course in Miracles are not that far out! What is far-out is to actually have an experience of communicating – only in the mind. Remembering, the Course was channeled through the mind – a concept acceptable to those who wrote the book. So, why not accept the concept two people can also communicate in spirit, (mind). Times are changing, you know!

6

ACIM & Einstein's E = MC ^{2}

What's Love got to do with it?

December 31, 2009

Dear Ken,

Once again, Christmas came and went with such gusto that it is now just another blip on the map of dreams. I will tell you that even without snow temperatures at the Mount Kelsey Estates dropped to 21 ^{0} forcing all to hover the fireplace cozy.

For me, Christmas is just Christmas. Not the birth of Christ, or the be-all-end-all of emotional gratifications: it is an opportunity to stop, at least one-time during the year, and remember each other. My two Arizona daughters could not make it, but we laughed and hugged over the phone. The moral of that repartee, it is good to have a change of scenery once-in-awhile!

Sorry, but Santa suits and blue snowflakes are not my idea of sexy! However, knowledge, intellect, infinite intelligence, thoughts, and real love are very sexy. Surely, you do not want me to think of you as sexy just when I am enjoying you metaphysically, you big-silly?

While Ewe fast-forwarded through the ethers and projected into your classroom as male: Eye came kicking and screaming through the vapors into my classroom as female. (okay, big deal - I came first)! Having arrived one is now expected to ignore the other — on the physical level — and work it out as one — on a metaphysical level? Wouldn't that have made Adam and Eve the first and last people on the planet! (Just checking). Hey! I'm grounded, remember?! You know I do not buy the Adam and Eve story, anyway.

Happy 2010, by the way.

One last bit of trivia, we (class) were going over whether facts speak for themselves when I found a comment that supports this thought. "Einstein's formula, $E = mc^2$ says Matter is Frozen Energy. What that means is that the understanding of a fact has other levels to which it can speak."

I like that. At first I thought that is a fairly elementary concept (?) that Matter is frozen energy. I could have thought of that, if I had just thought of it! Easy for me to say, after Einstein pondered over this for 20 years and almost did not come up with it first. Now, that is cheeky of me but, I am thinking it sounds simple because it makes sense. Not the formula as much as understanding a fact has other levels to which it can speak.

That could apply to ACIM by accepting the facts and understanding that facts have other levels to which a fact can speak.

You are so adorable on The Decision Maker CD, especially your take in the "quirky" character, perhaps because I can relate to quirky? I love that CD! p.s. Einstein would have classified you as my Cherished Sexy Friend. (Plato, too! Wise guy).

"I like your Einstein thing, but would you still like me if I take it one step further: Matter is frozen guilt. (Now we're talking!). I'm glad you like my adorable, quirky self. Do you think I should listen to that CD?" (Wapnick, 2010).

Einstein Theory of Relativity ~ E = MC²

Einstein's popular equation, $E = MC^2$ translates to: E ~ energy, M ~ mass, and C^2 represents the speed of light – squared.

1) **Energy** – thermal, electrical, and nuclear are the most popular forms of energy. Energy can be moved from one systems to another, it cannot be either created

or destroyed – it can only take different forms. Coal is potential energy when it is burned and turns into thermal energy.

2) **Mass**, the energy of any object times the square of its velocity or the speed of light.

3) **Mass** is the amount of matter found in an object and should not be confused with weight: weight is the gravitational force - mass is the amount of matter in that object.

4) **Mass** must be physically altered to change, whereas weight changes according to the gravity surrounding it.

5) **Mass** is weighted in kilograms (kg) while Neutrons (N) are the measurement for weight.

6) **Mass**, like energy can change form, but it cannot be created or destroyed. An example would be ice – in its melted state ice has the same mass as in its frozen state.

7) **Mass** and **Energy** are equivalent – they will tell you how much energy is in the mass. A little mass can hold a large amounts of energy (Wiki, 2016).

Now that the above is clear what does it mean you may ask. We learned early on that everything we can see consists of molecules (seen), and everything unseen consists of atoms. It takes two or more atoms to make a molecule.

Quantum Physics: a detailed study of everything in the cosmos starting with atoms (no-see-ums) and moving downward to subatomic particles, (Danes, n.d.).

When an atom is broken down to subatomic particles it consists of Photons, Leptons, Electrons, Neutrons, and, Quarks, etc. Why Einstein's 1925 Theory $E = MC^2$ was so profound, especially for his time, is because his scientific discovery proved atoms broken down to subatomic particles, could be further broken down to their most basic form or - pure vibrating energy – Light! (Danes, n.d.),

Light - Everything originates from this pure energy, meaning: We really are the Light of the World. As romantic as this may sound it also means We are responsible for the lives we live, the positive and the negative – yep – we create everything with our thoughts! A scientific fact, not just a good way to inspire people.

Since we originate from pure vibrating light, we are all connected at the origin of our pure existence – light. A confirmation of A Course in Miracles concept – we are One, in spirit, (Light). According to the Bible the first thing God created - Light. (Let there be light). The last thing individuals see after taking their last breath - Light - at the end of the tunnel (reported by Near Death Experience (NDE) survivors). As such, this suggests there is no limit to our potential to communicate in spirit once we understand our abilities and accept the process.

"When spirit's original state of direct communication is reached neither the body nor the miracle serves any purpose" (T-1, V-1:2). If neither the body nor the miracle serves any purpose – what is left but Light! Suggesting, light (our origin) has or is what is referred to as "Infinite Intelligence" through which we project our thoughts? (When Apple gets this there will be no more plugs or towers for our iPhones and computers)!

Now, as One in spirit where our minds are joined with spirits original state of direct communication: we would be much like subatomic particles able to communicate faster than the speed of light even when split in two as mentioned in Bohm's findings, (Danes, n. d.). Thus, the next step would be learning how to develop this amazing potentiality and communicate, at will, such as Ken communicates with me.

Back to subatomic particles - I like to refer to these particles as - pixels of the original. Picture this: what if each individual is like a pixel of the original Source – call it light, holographic visioning – or infinite intelligence? Same mind, divided (pixelated) into zillions of individuals. It is possible to break a photograph down to pixels, and then using these pixels to rebuild the original photo, ending the process. We have all seen the oil portrait - when viewed up close the whole portrait is a compilation of pixels of the original. Just like us!

Whereas, Ken is the only one I know who has the ability to move from one dimension and back at will, I believe this is available to everyone after we understand it exists and choose to develop our abilities. It is also possible this is not the only form of communication we will eventually become aware of.

Breaking it down further so I can understand this concept, I liken direct communication with spirit to the air we breathe. Oxygen is available to everyone, without question. We blindly accept what research has reported as to where it comes from and our use of air – it just is! The same can be said for communicating in spirit - it is available to everyone, just as the air we breathe – it just is!

For some reason, the population takes the air we breathe for granted, while assigning the possibility of communicating in spirit to a chosen few. Could it be more a matter of vibrational levels, and the fact it is possible to ignore the potential to communicate in spirit and still exist, while our ability to breathe air is essential to our existence?

It is a scientific fact everything has a vibrational level, humans, animals, plants, and even rocks, everything! It is more likely communicating in spirit is just another level of vibrating energy individuals are tuned into – depending upon the individual's energy. Perhaps, some come by this ability naturally, or become aware of the potential and study to develop the ability. What is certain, denying the potential to communicate in spirit exists, does not mean you have successfully erased the ability to communicate in spirit!

Basic Scientific Facts:

1) Vibrating light is unlimited and sends out wave forms of probability, which convert into subatomic particles:

2) Subatomic particles have the ability to communicate with each other at the speed of light even if split in half, (Danes, n.d.).

3) It takes two or more subatomic particles to create an atom.

4) Lastly, it requires two or more atoms to create a molecule and everything that can be seen is created with molecules: including humans, meaning – all of us have the potential to communicate in spirit depending on one's level of energy!

When ACIM reiterates we are One – in spirit – it acknowledges our potential to communicating in spirit, also. Thus, the choice to accept or deny our potential to communicate in spirit is a personal decision, rather than a lack of scientific fact.

What about the mind, if we are mind in a body, not a body with a mind, where does mind or memory fit into the equation? Currently, the mind and memory are considered to be two different entities: science has determined memory comes from the frontal lobe of the brain (Short version learned from my head injury). However, Edgar Cayce could recover memory (information) by tapping into the Akashic Record (AR), a holographic collar surrounding the universal illusion.

Many individuals do not believe in the AR either, which is okay, except it worked for Cayce. While in a trance Cayce could find individuals in their home, direct them to a medicine cabinet with instructions on what to do with a specific bottle on a certain shelf, instruct the entity to combine it with another substance to cure their affliction: all by tuning into the Akashic Record: it must mean something. Perhaps this could be considered 'a layer' of Einstein's Theory: $E = MC^2$ - or a variable to any given fact.

BTW Cayce was told to only do two sessions a day. One in the morning and one in the afternoon. However, he was so generous he increased his sessions until he reached the point where his own energy was drained – and this is what killed him, (History Channel, 2016).

As a child asking how many God's are up there anyway – may be answered by understanding religions are a concept developed by man while trying to understanding our reason for existing: and not based on any scientific fact. Just because each religion has their own version of their God, does not prove there is more than one God – or more than one source of our origin.

Personally, I accept the fact the source of everything is pure vibrating light, (Spirit?), (with Infinite Intelligence - God?), sending out wave forms of probability which convert to sub-atomic particles: sub-atomic particles become atoms, and two or more atoms become molecules. When the body dies the mind returns to pure vibrating light (spirit). This is an Eternal cycle that repeats itself into Infinity ~

Plus, where we are in our belief system also depends on our individual vibrating energy - another level of $E = MC^2$. Einstein's Theory of Relativity also supports A Course in Miracles concept we are one – in spirit, by taking the atom back to its basic source of vibrating light – the source of everything.

Thoughts:

Another question I had as a child and what led me to give up on religions: We were told the earth was 5,000 years old (?). Now updated to millions of years old: the automobile was invented give or take 125 years ago: What the hell were humans doing for all those years in between – unless it has all been done before? We don't know what we don't know, however Einstein's Theory has stood the test of time since 1925. Why $E = MC^2$ is so profound is because it explains the universe scientifically. Science is as close as humans can come to proving anything, plus it makes sense on a logical level. The source of everything is pure vibrating light, and it is Eternal.

7

Kenneth Wapnick Ph.D. & Freud

The "Love cure" a form of Psychotherapy
(Diamond, 2011, 2015).

$\mathcal{T}$here was a uniqueness about Kenneth Wapnick, Ph.D. as nearly everyone who came in contact with him felt the love. I would go so far as to say those who did not immediately feel this love had issues with their own self-importance, and not from anything coming from Ken. Then again, what I knew of Ken came from his letters, or from spiritual contact and not from frequent visits to the Foundation.

What does this have to do with Freud? For one thing: Freud was the founding father of Psychoanalysis – a method used to explore human behavior – a process Freud often referred to as the "Love Cure." He believed we are unable to explain our behavior to ourselves or to others, and are more adept in disguising the real reason for our behavior. Freud believed if you let a person talk long enough without judging, the patient would eventually solve their own problems. He provided comfortable surroundings, a couch for his patients and allowed them to talk about themselves.

Kenneth Wapnick, Ph.D. a Clinical Psychologist, had a passion for understanding human behavior going back to high school when he began listening to Beethoven. When introduced to A Course in Miracles he felt like 'he was reading it from the inside.' Like Freud, Ken encouraged me to write about anything that popped into my head.

Somewhere near the beginning of our letters I began to explain my childhood of abuse and neglect. Example: the reason I was terrified of water went way back. My birth was an inconvenient addition to her responsibilities. Thus, probably out of frustration, she held my head under my bath water for periods of time. This began at birth and continued until I was old enough to fight back. This produced convulsion each time I saw my bath water. No surprise, I grew up with a fear of water. As an adult and once I connected the near drownings with my fear of water the fear subsided. I still do not like water or participating in water games or slides.

There were two reasons I discontinued reporting on my childhood, 1) (Boring!) I had already resolved everything I could recall during the years after my only son was killed, 2) I did not wish to take advantage of Ken's professional advice without going through the professional channels.

Freud was the first to document the goal of Psychoanalysis as a way to make the unconscious conscious by breaking down the Psyche into three entities: Id: Instinct (our sub-conscience), Reality: ego, and the Superhero: Morality. The ego develops from the Id during infancy and functions in both the conscious and sub-conscious mind. Freud's Superhero: Morality was expressed by the infant identifying with the same sex parent and learning their sexual identity through that parent.

To make the unconscious conscious sounds similar to how ACIM teaches us to recognize the right mind (unconscious/subconscious) from the wrong mind (conscious/ego) and the decision maker where we make the choices.

Dr. Wapnick, taught A Course in Miracles by using these three components of our mind. The issue is to learn to spend more time in the right mind where we experience inner peace, and less time in the ego where we think we are living in this conflicted world of illusions. Dr. Wapnick reminds us we are either in the right mind or the wrong mind because we cannot be a little bit in both. When we catch ourselves in the ego we can return to the decision maker and choose again.

By any standards, an infant should never be left home alone for any reason. Too young to walk, I was left alone on a double bed during the day. This must have been known in the neighborhood because the mailman fed me through the window each day as he made his rounds. Freud's idea of the infant identifying with the same sex parent is not helpful when the only parent was seldom home, perhaps why I never bonded with my mother. I knew who she was but she could have been the checker in a super market for all I knew of her.

Freud was called ahead of his time for his insight. Dr. Wapnick was one of a kind for his passion and ability to interpret the Course. Freud's lifetime goal was to find a way to break through the barriers people erect for themselves so they can get to the source of their angst. Dr. Wapnick reminds us the Course gives us the tools to catch ourselves when in the ego and return to the right-mind by forgiving ourselves for forgetting we are One with God. In the process all barriers are removed and peace is restored.

Both Freud and Dr. Wapnick had Jewish parents during an era when it was not popular to be Jewish. Both were interested in the difference between religion and spirituality. Freud dealt with the nature of religious beliefs in many of his books. A Course in Miracles was channeled by Jesus and often amplifies religious stories from the Bible to validate the benefits of the Course. Freud believed God was an illusion and suggests religion was an attempt to control. The Course teaches the universe is an illusion because it is forever changing, and we are in control of the decisions we make. Anything of God is constant, changeless, and eternal (Nothing real can be threatened. Nothing unreal exists. Herein lies the peace of God (x-2, 1).

It took 10 years after the death of my only son to figure out my basic issues stemmed from a lack of love from my mother. The death of my son also taught me I did not have to grow in the direction of my mother, who never overcame her own issues as the middle child. She was resentful, spiteful, and competitive, and took it to her grave. She never let me know she loved me. The Gift left by my son was to remind me I had choices: whine my way through life like my mother, or open my eyes to discover my purpose in life. How and where we were born is not as important as what we do with this life once we get here.

Dollar-A-Day Child

My mother never explained why I was sent away to foster care. I was right out of a 10 day stay in the hospital after a tonsillectomy, and just before my third birthday, when she dropped me at my first care home. (Could have been a good thing as there was at least someone home with me). My first home was a farm full of animals and a barn with a rope swing hanging above a giant hay stack. It could have been a wonderful place to live, however that was not to be.

The family had twin daughters about my age and a five-year-old son. My introduction to the family was a game of sliding down the back of the bath tub, run around the corner to the kitchen for a soda cracker and back to the tub. As I entered the bathroom with my soda cracker one of the twins shoved me down, and ran. I struggled up too late to shove her back, and shoved the other twin who was closer. Unfortunately, this twin was eating her cracker and ---- she choked and died.

I was immediately removed from the home and grew up thinking I was a murderer. That must be why I was passed on to other homes, because the family I was with found out I murdered Martha. (When I was 50 I asked my mother if people thought I was a 'bad seed' or if they realized it was an accident? She laughed, and was surprised I still thought about it. Than told me she would call the mother and tell her because 'she would get a kick out of that?').

My foster care was not through the proper channels of going through the system: in fact, I am not sure there was a government program for the care of unwanted children during those years. My placements were within my mother's church. There were occasions when I would leave one home and not having a place to go so simply left home alone. Then, the following weekend we would be invited to lunch after church and while playing with other children my mother would disappear and that would be my home until the next time. For some reason I never connected lunch with a new home until years later when I recognized the pattern.

When I was five and going into my fourth home, I found myself on a ranch with a family who had four teenage children of their own. The youngest was a 14-year-old girl. The kids had chores but I was considered too little to participate. After an early breakfast I was strapped in a saddle on the back of a pony and led to the pasture gate where the father opened the gate, give the pony a swat on her rump, and off we would gallop into the pasture. The gate was closed and locked until lunch time when someone came looking for me, usually finding me in the barn, still strapped on the pony. (practical farmhouse babysitting). For which they were paid a dollar-a-day!

The good part was this family had a piano and every chance I had I sat at the piano and copied the names of the notes from a chart onto the church hymnal. Then compared the hymnal to the piano and in the process I taught myself to play the piano.

From the beginning of my foster homes experience I found solace by finding Orion in the night sky. Why Orion, I have no idea. What does a three-year-old know about Orion? When sad or feeling alone I would wait for the dark and find Orion. As an adult thinking back to those days it makes me smile as I recall calling Orion my home. Do I hear, Quirky? (I still do this, by the way???).

Not even teaching myself to play the piano by the age of five was good enough for my mother. By six I was accompanying the church pastor on his violin during church services – not good enough. The school bought a cello for me when I was eight and I joined the school orchestra – not good enough – graduated Valedictorian from eighth grade – not good enough! Sent away to boarding school and finally out of her hair.

Want & Windfall

After graduating Valedictorian eighth grade my ex-step-grandfather showed up at my grandmother's home with gifts. I had not seen him since I was two years old and viewed him as a stranger.

65

His name was Patrick, however I had no idea what to call him. Mr. Grandpa, Patrick, Pat, so I did not call him anything. His appearance and departure was so sudden it did not become an issue. I thanked him for the gold watch and cash and then he left.

Mr. Pat reappeared during the Christmas Holidays the year I turned 16. In his hat and top coat he made an impressive figure: so when he took me to the Chevrolet Dealer I followed meekly along. This was only the second time I had seen him since my infancy and what was happening was surreal. He paid cash for a baby blue Chevy Coupe telling me, knock the fenders off and bash the doors, and when you learn to drive I will buy you an Oldsmobile!

In the process he told me a story about having 14 oil wells in escrow for when I turned 18. It made no more sense to me than if he had said he would fly me to the moon! (After all, up to this point I was still making my clothes out of empty feed sacks). My car had just arrived by train and would not be ready for pick-up until after the weekend. PaPa Pat returned to Texas and his oil wells leaving me to pick up my Chevy!

Since I had never driven a car before the dealer took me for a ride to point out the functions of my new toy. I asked if it was okay if I drove it? He laughed and told me of course, since it was my car. Next, I proceeded to visit everyone I knew and introduced them to my gift. Piling on a record 170 miles in one day and never leaving the City limits!

In those days, girls did not have cars. What few boys had cars had old clunkers. No 16-year-old girl had a car, let alone a new car! It became normal to return to my car and one or more of the boys had tinkered with it so it would not start. I quickly learned how to replace the rotor and reconnect spark plugs.

Three days later, without a Driver's License or insurance, I drove back to boarding school with two friends. Why their mother's let them ride with me I will never know because I drove like a crazy wild woman laughing all the way. We were late arriving at the Girls Dorm after finding a couple of soldiers in Monterey and having a few giggles. The Principal decided to send me home for returning late when we could have been on time, plus no Driver's license. (I could return when I had a Driver's License and told him I was sorry!). They kept my car and delivered me to the bus station.

It took six-weeks before I had my Driver's License and could find someone to drive me back to school. When I returned to school they treated me as if I had committed a mortal sin. I was so embarrassed I drove back home. Years passed – at 27, after three husbands and five children, I went to the local high school on campus and earned my high school diploma.

Upon my return, my grandmother decided she had enough and no longer wanted me staying with her. I found a job in a Soda Fountain and went to work for 75 cents an hour. Too shy to wait on customers, and having been taught we were not to mingle with 'worldly people' I made sodas, milkshakes, and washed dishes. (plus, slept in my car for a month).

It was difficult to find a place to live on my salary. You would think Mr. Pat would come to my rescue and take care of my basics. After all, you have to groom a person to take over 14 Oil Wells! I did not have a way to contact him and too shy and embarrassed to search for him.

At 17 I solved my problems of not having a place to live by running off and marrying a divorcee with two children. And then - I heard from Grandpa! He did not approve of my marriage, even though I married the only child of the wealthiest family in town. Something to do with my husband's grandfather. It really did not matter – because he had cancelled my oil wells and left town!

After my third divorce and struggling to raise five children on my own, I was experiencing a love/hate relationship with religion. I wanted my children to be familiar with the Bible stories, but not be exposed to the church's list of sins. When the church began pounding sins into my oldest child we quit going to church. Mostly, I viewed church as an opportunity to show my mother what beautiful and well behaved children I had produced. Funny thing, she never acknowledged me, or my children at church, but I made sure she saw us!

Without communicating with me my mother sent the pastor to 'bring me back into the fold.' A friendly chap, the pastor knew better than to mention religion since I had slammed the door on him the first time he tried to visit. Eventually, we became civil and when he invited us to a church picnic at the Country Club, I accepted on the premise it was scheduled to be a beautiful day, good food, and fun for the children: **and no preaching!** As mentioned, the event turned out to be a disaster as my only son was killed while walking a back-road home with a friend. I did not go to church again for 30 years.

By the time Ken and I began communicating I felt like I had resolved the issues of my childhood. I believed you have to go back and go through it to get over it. So, I went back and sorted out events from an adult's perspective and realizing, for one thing, I was not a three-year-old murderer. It was instead, a terrible childhood accident. (no one ever bothered to console me, at the time) Whereas, the event can be pulled up from my memory forever, the pain it produced is gone.

Ken never referred to the "Love Cure" used in Freud's articles. In retrospect, I suppose it would qualify as such, since the process was similar. In an interview with Susan Dugan,

Ken relates his background was influenced by Beethoven while in high school. The more he listened to Beethoven's music the more he could feel the real heart of the music, and as he continued to listen to Beethoven the closer he came to the process.

I can relate to that because I learned to figure things out without giving it a name. If I came across something similar with a name it helped to identify the conclusion I had already accepted. By the time I began to explore A Course in Miracles I was already used to the fact religion per se was not for me.

By then, I was involved in discovering my spirituality. This is what I called a Gap. I had given up on religion, but had not yet filled the gap that left in my life. Whatever I had learned about spirituality I had yet to come across a theory I could trust or relate to until becoming involved with A Course in Miracles.

When I wrote to Ken for clarification on a comment in the Course, I had already become mesmerized by the concepts of the Course. However, what I did not know and only realized after we began corresponding, was the additional benefits of communicating in spirit! That was a huge surprise, and not in the ACIM Manual. I do not recall Freud ever mentioning this aspect of the Love Cure, although I have not read everything written by Freud.

Still, I am prone to say although Ken incorporated love in his process, he went far beyond just listening and sending love for his cure. Like Ken with Beethoven's music, he knew what was missing and went to the heart of things by teaching true love is the love of God.

Until recently, I did not know Freud used this "Love cure" or the transference of love. Perhaps this could apply to Ken's letters, however I believe Ken was original enough to develop his own process according to the client's needs. It is true Ken was fond of Freud, going back many years, it is also not unusual to assimilate concepts that resonate, especially when they coincide with A Course in Miracles.

Reflecting on my connection to Ken, I became bored with relating more stories about my loveless childhood. Believe me - there are many more stories. Times were different then. Besides, I realize there are hundreds of adults with worse stories than mine. In fact, the prisons are full of men who never experienced a mother's love and chose to join a gang as kids and up the ante as adults. If you want to see a grown man cry, ask him about his relationship with his mother. Those who are honest will easily tear-up. Meaning – they never overcame the lack of love and support from their mothers, real or perceived. Most likely, they never connected the lack of love to their life of crime...

When I mentioned two years into our letter writing how Ken <u>was</u> the Gift I had prayed for: it took his passing before I connected with the process. Ken's unconditional-love, steadfast and true, stayed with me, supporting me, like a mother's love should (which I never knew), until my heart absorbed his essence where I could return his unconditional love. He held me close (on paper) until we became one – in spirit.

It must be so as the steps leading to today constantly led in the same direction:

After having been fired for taking my screenplay to a studio on my day off I spent months exploring multiple religious philosophies, 2) which led me to A Course in Miracles (ACIM), 3) Soon, I became the facilitator for ACIM after the current one moved, 4) the only thing constant after the bus struck me was my position as facilitator for ACIM, 5) as facilitator a connection opened to the ACIM Foundation and thus my question for Ken, 6) Ken simply did what he was sent here to do: "Teach only love for that is what you are," (T-6. I.13:2).

Ken was just being, Ken – which to me was large. In more recent letters I apologized to Ken for not giving anything in return. How I involved him in my convoluted living adventures, through various incompetent doctors, taking him with me to court over a ticket for driving with a suspended license, Worker's Comp attorney dragging out my case for his benefit causing my homeless state to begin with. His response:

"You have given me everything! Thank you for caring enough to stay with me on your journey," (Wapnick, 2012). (Who thinks like this, for Pete's sake?).

Through the years, I often marveled over my accidental and unlikely connection to Kenneth Wapnick, Ph.D. Of all the individuals I had come across in my 70 years prior to Ken, who would ever suspect it would be Ken I connected with? What about relatives whom I have never met? Why not a few of them stepping up and finding my family? My maternal grandmother was the youngest of eight children, so there must be a number of lost relatives out there, somewhere.

There were times when I pondered how fortunate for me Ken could not see me and realize I am no longer young and cute: only to learn he travelled between dimensions and found me anyway! To add to the mystery, had I been harboring a desire to meet and become acquainted with Ken, would have been one thing. However, it never crossed my mind. Ken, to me was the kind of person one admired from a distance and remembered to mind your P's & Q's if ever in his presence.

When I wrote the first letter to Ken it was purely for information, and not a lure of some sort. I would rather fight a cage full of hungry alligators than take a chance on being rejected while going after the Untouchable!

What made it possible was the fact we communicated through letters. From my perspective the correspondent could have been anyone as he was non-threatening and friendly; like a big brother. Like Ken said about my accident; it is not that it happened, it is how you deal with it that counts.

Our letters began shortly after my accident and lasted through six years of the trauma of recovery, relocating, homelessness, and finally; Graduation and Las Vegas. Ken's support was with me during one of my darkest experiences ever and kept me focused. In the process he taught me, by example, to look up and see the Light! How can you not love someone who never, ever gave up on you, plus, never asked for anything in return?!

This is exactly why I agreed to write our story: to demonstrate the power of Unconditional Love. While I had Ken's loving support to get there, it is also possible to discover Unconditional Love on your own, with the help of the book, A Course in Miracles.

The ability to remain peaceful while the world is in turmoil is no small gift. Sad or unhappy you will learn how simple it is to correct yourself and move forward without guilt: plus, the use of it is available to everyone. It is not magic: our situations follow our thoughts. It is *your* choice! As Ken used to say, "You cannot mess this up!"

A Tribute to Gloria Wapnick ~

As Ken was my support, Gloria was Ken's support. She devoted her life to Ken by providing the platform he needed to become the Legend he became. Unique in her position as the supportive wife of a husband who most everyone loved: and who loved everyone in return! She was Eve to his Adam, Alpha to his Omega, and Mozart to his baton. One of a kind, and a role model for other wives. Gloria deserves our respect! When she offered her garage as Ken's platform, all those many years ago, little could she have known how this gesture would play out. My Love reaches out to Gloria...

Thoughts:

Everyone has a story! While mine is unique to me, it is no more important than another individual's story. If left to me, Ken's letters would still be in the box. However, Tamara enlightened me in two ways, 1) There are actually Course students who are unaware of Ken's playful side, 2) my story can be helpful to those who did not realize the potential to communicate in spirit can be achieved by using concepts from A Course in Miracles.

Fortunately, I now agree because the results of our story could also give a platform for others who have experienced communicating with Ken, in spirit. The results could also be an increase of new students who want to learn how to communicate in spirit, too!

With the way technology is going, i.e. moving a prosthetic limb with the mind: learning the process of communicating in spirit could become a valuable tool.

8

Chunky Monkey

Love and Forgiveness

*T*he use of Chunky Monkey in our conversations started as a play on words over Ken's comment as to why he thought he was Monk material. It evolved into meaning Love and Forgiveness. I originally used it and Ken changed the use of it! Just as holy-moly was my ottoman where Ken first appeared in spirit, Ken changed the meaning of Holy-Moly to our Little Garden where we met on a regular basis.

When things appeared to me in dream state and later came across in my waking state Ken told me there is nothing wrong with going about my daily business while still on the Holy-Moly! (Right Mind). While I slept the image of two slim blue vases, sitting side-by-side in a window and back lit by the sun appeared to me. They were so vivid just the thought of them brought up the images even after I was awake and taking care of business.

Later, in the day I walked into my favorite antique shop and saw the same two slim blue vases sitting side-by-side on a glass case backlit by light streaming in through the window. Or while 'sleeping' I see myself lounging on a bed of red rose petals surrounded by white dahlias – it is so peaceful I open my eyes to see if I was dreaming and they were still there. I close my eyes again and they are still there. I took this as a good sign, but was not sure until Ken said I was going about business in my right mind.

Another time, while driving up a windy canyon road that dropped off on the left hundreds of feet into the river below, a vivid picture of a red vehicle speeding around a blind curve on my side of the road appeared in my head. Taking this as an alert I slowed as I came to the next right turn on a blind curve, nothing! The following curve was a sweeping left turn with a glorious view of the area followed by another blind curve. As I cautiously approached the blind curve a red car came speeding around the corner on my side of the road while passing another vehicle!

If I had not 'seen' this scenario I would have been traveling faster and could have been struck by the red car. Now, I called it Ken because my situation was stressful at the time and Ken seemed to be closer when I was under stress. Also, Ken did say there was nothing wrong with going about business while still on the Holy-Moly! (Another example of an experiences I did not know could happen to me…).

I understand those who may suspect I am losing my grip – that would be me, too – at one time. What I called 'quirky' was an extension of my desire to get to the truth. Why my letters were always testing Ken – not because it was my job, which it was not – but because I was hopeful Ken was promoting the truth even when challenged. Did I see myself as qualified to do so, no! Just past experiences had taught me to be on the alert for hidden agendas.

The results proved we are all capable of these experiences – it only requires learning to become aware when we have a feeling or a sighting, pay attention. The test of true love is in the ability to meet in the mind, not in the physical contact.

Although the two of us never discussed this, Ken was always way ahead of me. He gave as good as he got, so to say! He was never cranky, never chastised me for my silly rhetoric, never withheld a letter to make a point, they always arrived in Thursdays mail.

Thoughts:

You may recognize Chunky Monkey as the flavor of one of Ben & Jerry's ice cream concoctions. It popped-up when Ken asked if I wanted to make 'sumthin' out of his idea to become a monk. I said if he did not want to talk about it have some Chunky Monk-ee and we can forget about it. (I love this ice cream).

Ken incorporated it to become Love and Forgiveness, and why not, that is the essence of the Course? Besides, it makes one smile when used – even if you do not understand the usage. It also demonstrates Ken's playfulness...

9

A Tribute to Ken

"If Gratitude is an Attitude, then my Attitude, is in the Altitude."

*O*nce, I asked Holy-Spirit what took me so long to recognize Ken was my Gift – the answer came swiftly, "My innocence was fetching!"

While Ken was still with us and communicating weekly with love and support, my creativity soared. My thoughts and personality catapulted, becoming 'frisky' and anxious to report to the paper within my computer screen. Some profound, some goofier than before, yet all visions of my potential. There are moments when I feel like a no-see-um surfing the white Light on my Hoverboard while joining with Ken in spirit. Other times, I see Ken everywhere reminding me we are one in spirit, equals.

This demonstrates how valuable a mother's love is to her child, even when we think they are 'too young to understand.' Children raised with unconditional love and support will excel in life, whereas those raised on the edge without the support of motherly-love, in particular, will go through life struggling to find their way.

My case as a foster child is classic: I can relate the difficulties of missing a mother's love. How my life was a constant struggle, I never fit in. By the time I could articulate my angst I had messed up my life. My only goal in life was to become a mother and have a family to belong to, after which we lived happily ever after! I accomplished this by marrying at 17 for a place to live, becoming an instant step-mother of two - a mother of four by 22 (the oldest not yet four). Remarried by 25 adding another child at 27. After this unlimited bliss, I spent the next 20 years raising my family – mostly alone.

Loren was killed on the 8th of October, in December I took a Christmas season job as cashier in a market. It felt good to be productive and when it was over I qualified for unemployment. At the time, those on unemployment had to pick-up their checks at the Employment Office. This involved standing in line with other recipients, plus you also had to bring a list of where you had searched for work (with phone numbers) since your last check in order to qualify for the current check.

At the window I asked the woman how I could get an even better job. For some reason I told her I was not the smartest person on the planet, however I was not the dumbest, either. She scheduled me for a test. The results: she claimed 'only 1% of the working nation was more intelligent than me.' She said someone would contact me, soon. Shortly, a man arrived at our home and told me I qualified for a four-year scholarship. They would also take care of my children, however he was leaving on a month vacation. We could go into the details upon his return.

Although I heard the words – things did not compute. One of the reasons I did not have a fulltime job was because the salary was $1.50 per hour and so was babysitting. It did not make sense to work just to pay a babysitter to raise my kids. Yet, here is someone offering to send me to university for a degree and take care of my children, too? But, I would not know the outcome for a month until he returned from his holiday! Did someone say, 'pass the butter?'

I will never know the outcome because 10 days later my best friend asked me to take her 15-year-old sister and cousin to the San Francisco Airport. As we entered the terminal a well-groomed, handsome man approached with a smile on his face and his hand outstretched holding his business card. He invited us for refreshments while waiting for the girl's flight. (He later admitted he liked my legs and went inside the terminal and around to see what I looked like from the front!). Bastard! ; >).

After asking where I worked and learning I was unemployed he referred me to his friend who owned an Employment Agency. Two days later I had a job with a Brokerage Firm in the accounting department for $350 a month. What does this have to do with anything - because it explains the difference between those who have missed out on a mother's love compared to those who were nurtured during infancy and early childhood. (bad decisions).

Once I became comfortable with my new job and the holidays were over, I decided I needed to thank the guy and report on my job. After all, he came into my life for two days and changed everything! He disappeared! It took 18 years to find him and he did not even remember me!

One may look at a successful person and wonder what is the difference between 'them & me?' The 'me' could even be better looking and smarter than the 'them.' To be successful requires the emotional level be equal to the intellectual level. If an individual is unable to back-up their intellectual quotient with an equally healthy emotional level life will always be a struggle. This requires a mother's love to gives the child the security needed to support their intellectual level.

Although it is possible to recover from having a weak emotional level it is important the individual recognizes what they are working with. It is not likely a grown man is going to say something like, 'My mommy didn't love me so I chose a life of crime!' It is also unreal to expect a child to ask for love from someone to make up for what they lacked at home. People just do not articulate this issue.

Those who are successful and write books about the power of positive thinking do not understand what the lack of a mother's love is like. So they promote things like; thinking positive, actualization, abundance, gratitude, and an assortment of other platitudes. There are plenty of readers who wonder how to become successful and buy books thinking this will solve their problems. Odds are it will help a few, and those left over will resort to their old ways of coping.

"Unless those who have insecurities holding them back happen to understand the need to balance the emotional with the intellectual, and set about to educate themselves, no one is going to magically appear and fix it for them." You cannot 'fix' the problem if you cannot even articulate the problem!

This all becomes very clear when the concepts of A Course in Miracles are understood. It is possible to balance the emotional with the intellectual by practicing the concepts of the Course. The central thread of the Course is that we are all one, or the same! We must learn to look to the love of God for our strength, and not commiserate forever over the loss of affection as an infant and small child. My theory is: if everyone understood the source of their emotional instability they would absolutely hunt for solutions. The best solution is A Course in Miracles.

In my letters to Ken I notice some of my reactions are those of a small child. On one-hand, I was the two-year old throwing tantrums (testing a mother's love) to run him off (or see if he would stay). On the other-hand, I am the senior citizen who has had enough of hidden agendas from men professing eternal love! Did I realize this at the time – Hell no! (as Ken would say!). It is a little embarrassing at the moment, since I thought I was smarter than that. However, I must applaud Ken for maintaining his professionalism and passing my tests!

It became clear Ken's letters were addressing the child within, the little girl searching for her mother's love. It was not the expected process where one pours out their heart to the therapist and the therapist then assures the individual they are loved, but come back next week! Rather, it was how Ken stayed with me until his *pure-love* and my 'lack of love' were united – the transference of love. Ken and his letters *were* my Gift!

What I prayed for repeatedly had arrived only I had not recognize the connection until it was too late to truly thank Ken! Why it took so long to recognize my prayers had been answered must have something to do with my expectations. Expectations are an act of anticipation – of a future event. This act of my attempts to orchestrate the future had limited my recognition of the present results. (Another Course concept – past and the future are the same).

The benefits of understanding the Course are profound, multiple – and non-threatening. We are here to discover our purpose. We are not expected to be perfect because if we were perfect we would not be here. We are also expected to take responsibility for our negative thought processes and forgive ourselves when we catch ourselves reacting to the ego. How could it be otherwise – either God is a loving God of True

Unconditional Love – or, He is not. If He is not, then he is as conflicted as we are and there is no God!

Dear Dr. Ken,

I hope you're fire proof? This surely has been an interesting week. The doors of opportunity opened, slammed shut, opened and slammed shut again, faster than the beat of a new drummer, with only one drum stick in a small towns marching band. ...and then a window flew open! I thank you. Thank You.

Joseph P. probably doesn't even realize how much help he turned out to be, He thought he was only referring me to a PI attorney who no longer operates from his firm; yet, in the process, in a fatherly way, he encouraged me to check on the damage claim to make sure it had been filed. I did, it hadn't and of 180 days only 30 were left! WHEW! God works in wondrous ways!

I so appreciate your willingness to communicate with me and offer support: you just being there is comforting. It's even more fun 'cause you don't know me. Gotta love ACIM!

"Don't know you???????????!!!!!! ' ! ??????????How silly is that??????!!!!???????
You're a Son of God, aren't you; sometimes silly, sometimes happy. Right? Who says I don't know you?" (Wapnick, 2007).

Thoughts:

We all know the past is past, and we all know the hazards of dwelling on the past, however there are also levels to this concept. I have discovered to go back to my childhood and review the events from an adult's perspective can dispel the pain of the events, real or perceived. For example: I grew up a shy child because of my interpretation of my situation. Shuffled from home to home meant my mother did not want me. If she did not want me there must be something wrong with me.

Children, especially small children tend to think they are the center of the universe. If parents fight, it must be their fault. If the picnic was fun, it is because they were there, etc. On this concept, going back and releasing the pain of one's upbringing can be therapeutic, and necessary to be able to move on.

Dwelling on the past is another thing. When I worked at the Fountain older men drank coffee and spent hours discussing their military days, over, and over. How that one adventure was all they had left. It made me realize it would be better to get out there and keep having more adventures instead of becoming stuck in the past.

Communicating in spirit is a whole new and different adventure!

10

Literary Hug for My Cherished Friend

"No one in my long and boring life has ever met me on the holy-moly."
(Wapnick, 2008).

Once upon a mind, where there is no time,
this little girl got lost.
Like you and me, she could not decide,
so on the waves, she had to ride.

She heard of this guy, who did all he could,
just to keep folks boats afloat.
So she sent out a note, onto which she wrote,
please tell me the truth, don't hide.

Before very long, a thought came along,
saying she was not alone.
She poured out her heart, to this gifted soul,
thinking how 'true love' she would never know.

He held her heart close, filling it with love,
returning to her, as a Gift from above.
Overwhelmed with joy, by one who taught her to love,
by visits to her mind.
She tells this story, of unconditional love,
to those he left behind.

We have come to the end, of my story about Ken,
who now is vibrating light.
Try as I would, not all is understood,
which I hope to resolve tonight.

Ken the body is gone, moved to the beyond,
while I live on - an old lady.
Before I go, it would be nice to know,
it is possible to share our journey.

Everyone has a right to know, there is much,
more to this spiritual love story.
When thinking of love, it is seldom the kind,
where two entities only meet in the mind.

While searching for true love, try looking above,
to the Light just out of reach.
If you knew True Love lasts forever,
would you trade it for the silly kind?
When Unconditional Love is of the Spirit
and thus, surely from the Divine!

(Rub-a-Dub-Dub, n. d.).

The Little Garden

"You have reached the end of an ancient journey, not realizing yet that it is over. You are still worn and tired, and the desert's dust still seems to cloud your eyes and keep you sightless. Yet He Whom you welcomed has come to you, and would welcome you. He has waited long to give you this. Receive it now of Him, for He would have you know Him. Only a little wall of dust still stands between you and your brother. Blow on it lightly and with happy laughter, and it will fall away. And walk into the garden love has prepared for both of you." (T-18, V-.III-13:1-8).

I am not a body. I am free. For I am still as God created me. (Lesson 2010.

"I do hope you forgive me for barging in on you that way. But I thought you'd be soundly asleep in bed, not on the ottoman, which borders on the sinful! I'm glad we could meet like that, Bunny. Maybe we'll do it again sometime. What do you say?" (Wapnick, 2008).

Melos

Ken was the Father I never had –
the Brother I wished for –
and showered me with the Love a mother is
expected to provide.
I will Forever Treasure my
friendship with Ken!

Thoughts:

Since Ken's passing not much has changed, except no more letters. However, Ken continues his visits and demonstrates in playful ways his approval of our book. When I became stuck, I awoke to find my two plain black dressers covered in red roses. I closed my eyes, they were still there. Opened my eyes, and yes, they were still there. Sharing our story has been bittersweet for several reasons. I am aware not everyone will be receptive to our spiritual love story because they are still thinking we are bodies.

Seasoned Course students will understand spiritual love is not of the body. In spirit where all are one we experience pure Unconditional Love. 'When spirits original state of direct communication is reached, neither the body, nor the miracle serves a purpose, (T-1. V-1:2). My story may activate others who have communicated in spirit with Ken, also. How Joyful that would be! I suspect there are those who will meet me and wonder, why her? I have pondered the same thing… Fortunately for me, the Course is not about the body!

Many *Thanks* to all who have joined with me on my Journey!

~ Memories ~

September 1 1, 2008

Dear Ken,

While others see this body, with your name on it, running around, teaching, etc., they may have no idea what this takes from you. I know I would be so happy to be in your presence, see your smiling face, listen to your kind words; it's possible it would take me awhile to think of a way to return this gift.

You did sound exhausted in your last letter, and yes-- I read your schedule in the Lighthouse, and noticed the Academy, and the three-day weekend were sequential. To recharge, is to reconnect; at least that is what I have to do with my cell phone.

Your playful comments make me smile out loud. You think I have led an interesting life, while it feels like I have spent my whole 'life' trying to make chicken soup, out of chicken s---! (maybe, I told you that before? That means it is true).

You, on the other hand, visited the Holy Land with Helen and Bill! (for Pete's sake!). I have wanted to visit Israel for ever-so-long, but thought I would wait for a significant other to show up because I know it will be emotional. Turns out, I over waited, and now it's too late.

September 24, 2009

Dear Kenneth,

Yes, yes, I miss you too, even though I listen to your sweet voice each morning after showering and while I take the palette to my face... It may be why it seems that we jabber each day. (?)

The sky is awash with your favorite color while the air shuffles along to the tune of my pet daffodils. I continue to search for something in purple, my other love... It is so tempting to share my thoughts with you, except you must have felt them on the holy-moly?

After a week with two-year old Zaydin, the incarnate of Attila-the-Hun, not sure what a stroke is, I adopted it and went to bed. It was not the merchant of bad news after all — so after a good nights sleep it was business as usual. I once thought that I had the child care gene, a mother earth — of sorts. Well, you can forget that!

He did leave some cuteness behind. Being a free spirit - I often had to tell him "NO" which he did not like. I would say, Zaydin, no-is-no. Wanting very much to continue with his mischief he would repeat, "no-is-no" and keep going. I asked, "Are you listening to me?" His reply, "Not listening to you" Well, no-is still-no and you better listen. At that point his dimples puddled into a big grin and away he would go.

(Cute, because no screaming or yelling, just logic).

The old-me (wait, would the old-me really be the young me?) must be returning, because I recently applied at the Colony Theatre, read your books daily, and see a few movies while I await the ceremonies dressed in cap and gown. ("They" would not let me pick my colors,...).

My attorney sent me to a psychiatrist because I told him I thought I had a stroke. In retrospect, I think I was tired, my left eye began to pin-wheel and I could not focus, finals were looming, and my take is I had a compound-fracture of my cheerful disposition, that's all!.

"And I concur with the diagnosis: no stroke, but a slight (and very temporary) fracture of your joyful right mind. But still we meet in the holy-moly." (Wapnick, 2009).

Dear Kenn,

Ahhhhhh! You get me every time in the P.S. line but it's such a good get!

And yes, there is something wrong with me — I will deny it as usual, except to you and my attorney; I still have double vision that makes things swim on the pages, sometimes it takes a minute for things to hold still, or it comes to me backwards first. Nothing hurts, so I just carry on. I do not always catch errors, like spelling, or sometimes my thoughts come backwards, Since I was born bum first it is really just more of the same old adjustments.

Are you fluent in French? If so, I shall try harder, and see how it goes on the holy-moly. Right now, I am stuck on — Enchante'. It sounds so deliciously Frenchy.

By the way, I see you in everything — why is that? Is it a result of the hit I took to my head in the accident? If I see you does it mean you are also seeing me, and what if I do not want you to see me? If I were to open my eyes in the shower and see you standing/hovering there I would slip on purpose and bang my head, again! (Sympathy may distract one's vision?).

What could be more fun than two silly 'no-bodies' slinking about in the ether of fantastic thought? Yes, I am goofy and not without good reason. How do you think I survived?

PS: By the way, what made you think you were "Monk" material — hmmmm!

"And of course if you are seeing me I'm seeing you. How could it not be since we is joined at the holymoly hip? As for my being a monk, I just liked it. Wanna make sumthin' of it?? ???! ! ! ! !!" (Wapnick, 2009).

October 23, 2009

Dear Kenneth,

You make me giggle! Sure, I'll make sumthin' out of your monk material. I thought it may have sumthin' to do with a female. (ha). Of that I can relate.

(Maybe not the female part). Try, Chunky-Monk—ee and we'll forget about it!

Do you realize that I am so bizarre there were times I thought your articles in the Lighthouse was directed at me to help me "live-it." If that is true, I thank you, if it is my imagination — please consider the source and understand my empirical evidence is in tune with the ethers, yet could skid off course on occasions. (like most of the time). This current issue seems to be an exception I did not get the same connections even though I can relate. (That would be my e-g-oh).

Do you have a lot of googly-eyed friends? It does seem to be a status symbol, One of many views. Uh oh, if one has double vision than that means our perceptions are double tooooooo. That will require a lot of work. Oy!

See you on our holy-moly—.

Nov, 3. 2009

Dearest Ken,

It took the loss of my son to understand that I am a loner (monk) and it's okay. It does seem to fit as I now like being alone. Besides, I have been divorced for over 39 years, while I wouldn't mind male companionship, I'm still alone.

Maybe, being alone is easier than being close to one person, (who might reject me). I now see where I tried to run you off, or maybe see if you would stay. You were way ahead of me — and I am grateful for your patience.

What's so different about this interpretation of my behavior? I finally get-it! What I was waiting for has been right there under my nose for two years while I took the Lolly-too-dums approach to our friendship. Now, I see where connecting with you on the holy-moly was like an introduction to help me get over thinking these things do not happen to me. When it was evident that I was not making it up, I came forward and acknowledged our connection. The magnitude has just now sunk-in. You may have to help me with this (?).

How will this change my life, I have no idea. Perhaps it will not change at all, on the outside. Hopefully, I will quit testing you and accept the Oneness.

You Take My Breath Away - was not for you as a come-on, although it wobbled on the line, and even confused me. Now, it fits a comfortable spot and I understand you already knew it.

Have I made any sense to you, at all, and could you explain it to me? (Enchante').

November 13, 2009

Dear Ken,

You must surely be aware of how beloved your Academies are, and how important they are to the students. Five days of morning and afternoon sessions are a gift only you can give.

No, you will never be my humble servant, but you will always be My Sunshine.

You are right to remind me one does not speak on the Holy-Moly — even I admit to only being aware of your essence, as if that is not enough! Cow-a- Bunga is my best reaction at the moment, while words have eluded me. (me? I know!).

I respect, and enjoy your supportive explanations — you Chunky-Monk-ey — you!

"Anyway, aside from an occasional Cow-a-Bunga, we shall continue our wonderful meetings on the Holy-Moly - in blessed silence. Thanks for shining your sun on me, dear." (Wapnick, 2009).

November 28, 2009

My first reaction to your confirmation was to think you could have helped me, then it would not have taken me so long! That must have been the ego over reacting to cover-up my embarrassment for being slow. In reality, it is suddenly obvious that it was you who sent the poem, "You Take My Breath Away"- met with me on the Holy-Moly — your essence appeared in my lucid dreams — followed me wherever I went, spoke to me in the Lighthouse, and never, ever gave up on me.

Thank you for never giving up on me.

References

1-Burley, B. (n. d.). The Throw-Away Child, A Personal Journal, by Bernyce Leone Burley – a.k.a. Bunny Moazed MS.

2-Danes, C. (n. d.). Quantum Physics - E=MC2. 7 Hidden Keys. www.AbundanceandHappiness.com

3-Diamond. S., (2015). Essential Secrets of Psychotherapy. www. Psychonogytoday.com.

4-McCants, G., (2008). Love By The Numbers

5-Schucman, H. (1976). A Course in Miracles. Foundation for Inner Peace. www.facim.org

6-Thompson, H. (n.d.). Rub-A-Dub-Dub Lyrics – MetroLyrics.

7-Wapnick, K. (2007-2012). Quotes from personal letters.

8-WikiHow, (n.d.). How to understand E= mc² - 7 Steps with Pictures. http/:www.WikiHow.com. Understand - E=mc²

9-Williams, K. (2014). How New Physics is Validating Near-Death Concepts. www.near-death.com/resources/artical. html.

Epilogue

$\mathcal{O}$n the 26th of July 2013, I moved to Las Vegas not realizing Ken was terminal. I wrote to him with my good news and received a letter from the ACIM Foundation informing me Ken was too ill to respond. My first reaction was one of complete suspension of all thoughts. You could have stabbed me in the heart and I would not have felt a thing. My options were few, except to try to connect in my mind. I felt lost, and at peace at the same time. Since I am older I just took the liberty to assume I would go first – or Ken would become bored with my goofy letters and discontinue our correspondence. My time had come without warning, I must carry on and be grateful for Ken's loving support and guidance over the past six years.

During the weeks following, I went through our letters and organized them in chronological order. Surprised by finding over 450 letters, I began at the beginning reading through one at a time. They were more meaningful on the second read than reading them while I was under stress of my situation. I found the letters joyful and entertaining – with a message in the *melos* not perceived earlier.

When Ken made his final visit the night before his official passing it never occurred to me to wonder how he found me in

Vegas. It was just Ken doing his thing. He seemed energized and happy, in his usual playful mood. Although his visit was rushed he managed to leave his love and grace behind. Nothing has changed, except no more letters. Ken still checks in on occasion – especially when I reach out to him.

In my solitude since Ken passed several things have connected, which I would like to relate. Do they mean anything – important? I suppose not. Just curious to me.

1. Ken passed shortly before he would have turned 72 – so did Helen.
2. Helen and my mother were born the same year - 1909 and the same month – July: Helen was 10 days older than my mother.
3. My brothers' name is Kenneth.
4. My mother's name was Lucile (Louie) Helen's husband was also Louie.
5. Ken liked numbers, so do I – his birthday is a double master number 2-22-1942.
6. My birthday numbers (not as strong as Ken's) 6-11-1936.
7. Both 11 and 22 are Master numbers – known for always having the feeling of "What's Next;" it keeps them in perpetual motion and forever getting ready for the next project, (McCants, 2008).

Reader's Guide

A broken neck from the May 19, 2007 accident ended the Author's driving career, income, and social life. After catching up on sleep it became obvious no longer having a purpose was becoming an issue. To get up each morning and back to bed every night left large gaps of unproductive opportunities, such as spending money you do not have on things you do not need.

The only function that remained constant was her commitment to facilitating *A Course in Miracles* study group once a week at Unity Church. An attempt to resolve the interpretation that every time we slip into our ego we perpetuate the illusion - a Course concept - led the Author to write the August 19, 2007 letter to Dr. Kenneth Wapnick asking for clarification. This random act initiated a series of over 450 letters during the next six years. (Eight months of her letters were left on the computer for safe-keeping, and lost when Microsoft crashed her computer while attempting to upgrade to Windows 10).

By the end of 2007 the Author had enrolled in online university classes giving her a purpose and furthering her education in the process. She selected Criminal Justice with the idea of becoming a crime scene investigator – a new career potential for post recovery. Her primary objective was to focus on improving loss of memory, concentration (no multitasking) and adjust to annoying double-vision. In the event she actually graduated amidst the process of recovery, she would have the benefit of a degree in her new field of interest! She attributes her connection to Dr. Wapnick as a catalyst and influence on her positive decision-making and recovery.

In March 2010 the Author began her homeless journey until the end of July F2013 when she moved into her own apartment in Las Vegas. It is often easy to see the stress in the letters although she is attempting to keep it from Dr. Wapnick. This creates redundancies of thought. Concepts already covered and resolved often resurface. Dr. Wapnick remains supportive.

Dr. Wapnick encourages the Author to make jokes about the ego, the Illusion, and to laugh at fearful misconceptions. In other words, do not give the ego any power – laugh, be silly. A total departure from his serious classroom persona.

The Author struggles in many sections to write light hearted letters and has a hard time doing so without dragging up the past. She knows better, yet it is less threatening than her current situation. She soon tires of reporting on her loveless childhood and never completes the whole story which she thought had been resolved long ago.

She is aware of the humor in writing to Dr. Wapnick, the premiere lecturer and teacher of *A Course in Miracles:* and the irony in reminding his students to recognize this world is an illusion – when she is seriously wounded and going through recovery while homeless making her situation seem *really* – **Real.** She is challenged to know what to write about, bring up the past – which does not exist, complain about her situation (in the illusion) - and make it real, or write about silly stuff, to take her mind off the situation. In the process she discovered

Dr. Wapnick has a silly-streak as well! Scattered throughout the silliness in the repartee between these two are tidbits of real information. Just enough to keep the letters flowing and the focus on the positive.

The year 2013 was a tough year for both. Dr. Wapnick is seriously ill and does not tell the Author, except in symbols which the Author overlooks. In one of her letters she speaks of taking care of the body so the mind has a stable classroom. This seems to indicate she was indeed aware, on some deeper level. The more recent letters are missing much of the playfulness of the earlier letters.

When Dr. Wapnick invited her to the Foundation in Temecula, CA, she refuses – telling him he would not recognize her, anyway! This tends to indicate the Author's frustration since at the time they had already been communicating in spirit and through the written word for over five years! Truth be known, Dr. Wapnick would have known instantly who she was! The Author was embarrassed by having missing teeth from the accident – and would have gone anyway had she known Dr. Wapnick was terminally ill. (A decision she will forever regret!).

The Author eventually admits to her given name – but tells Dr. Wapnick even her computer underlines it in red, meaning *no such word*. Also, her given name is the street name for cocaine – and likely why this name is never given to a newborn. Dr. Wapnick reminds her what a beautiful name it is while the Author continues to sign-off as usual. By the time the Author accepts Dr. Wapnick's many suggestions to use her given name he is too ill to acknowledge or respond. Both lives are transitioning.

The Author wrote Dr. Wapnick advising him of her move to Los Vegas the end of July 2013; However, her letter was

103

returned with a note informing her Dr. Wapnick was too ill to respond. Even without this information Dr. Wapnick appeared in her Las Vegas apartment during the early morning hours the night before his official death on December 27, 2013. As she lay sleeping in the shadows, He held her face in both hands, and kissed her on the lips, waking her. She yelled, "Stop that!" than realized it was Dr. Wapnick – and begged him to return. However, Dr. Wapnick was on a fast track to Eternity. He left behind a room full of peace and Unconditional Love.

Although the Author no longer receives a letter from Dr. Wapnick each Thursday, he still checks in occasionally with love and support, especially when the Author reaches out to him.

About the Author

The Author's childhood was a constant series of moves from one foster care home to another. By the time she graduated eighth-grade she had been in the care of 11 families. The first thing she did as a child moving from home to home was search the night sky for Orion. For some reason Orion was her comfort zone. In her mind, that was her home. Now, how and why this was her comfort zone, she always laughs and says, "that is where she came from."

She credits a sense of humor as her ability to have survived the neglect and lack of love from her parents. In addition, she never grew 'roots' because of her multiple home situation.

As a child she made 'books' for her doll, and prayed each night her doll would be a baby sister when she awoke in the morning. Although the baby sister never appeared, she did become the mother of four beautiful daughters!

She has no regrets over her four marriages, recognizing she chose men with similar issues, which she thought she could 'fix!' From these unions came a son (deceased) and four beautiful daughters, all successful professional business women.

Through the years, the Author had a variety of employments that served to care for her family. A Brokerage Firm, Model Agency in San Francisco, Bank Trust Officer, Bookstore Owner, Limousine Chauffeur for 20 years, and numerous volunteer opportunities.

She always regretted not furthering her education, and proud of her accomplishments with only a High School diploma. The accident was the catalyst that allowed her to earn her Associates and Bachelor's Degree in Criminal Justice. She went on to graduate summa cum laude with a Master of Science Degree in Administration of Justice and Security. The top three professions she is qualified for are: Sheriff, Judge, or work in Aerospace: in addition to having been inducted into the Criminal Justice Honor Society as Alpha Phi Sigma.

The Author acknowledges it was not likely she would have met Dr. Wapnick if not for the accident. While Dr. Wapnick tells her he did not send the bus, however it did slow her down so he could 'catch up with her!' Spirit works in marvelous ways!

Printed in the United States
By Bookmasters